The Secret of
Butterflies

シークレット・オブ バタフライズ

大坪　奈保美

Hakusan Creation
www.hakusancreation.com

© 2024 Naomi Otsubo and William Ash
All rights reserved. Published 2024

Translation by Naomi Otsubo and William Ash
Design, photographs, and illustrations by William Ash

ISBN: 978-1-935461-11-1 (Hardcover, Japanese and English)
ISBN: 978-1-935461-12-8 (Paperback, Japanese and English)
ISBN: 978-1-935461-13-5 (eBook, Japanese)
ISBN: 978-1-935461-14-1 (eBook, English)

Printed in the United States of America

Cover photograph: Library of Congress, *Nagasaki, Japan after atomic bombing / U.S. Army A.A.F. photo*. Nagasaki Japan, 1945. Photograph. https://www.loc.gov/item/91482332/

Contents

 親愛なる両親とアゲハに捧ぐ

In memory of my parents and butterflies

Chapter 1

　4、5歳の私は、母と一緒に、病院のような白いビルの中にいた。ビルの中は清潔で、明るかった。大きな敷地にポツンと立っていて、周りは高い壁に囲まれていた。幼い私は、そのビルに馴染みがあるようで、のどかな気持ちで廊下を歩いていた。

　突然、母が私の手を引いて、ビルの外に出た。そして門まで来ると、私を門の外に押し出して門を閉め、ビルの中へと戻って行ってしまった。母は、何も言わなかった。

　当たりは真っ暗で、誰もいなかった。一人残された私はただ怖くて、母の名を呼びながら泣き出した。

「また怖い夢を見たの？」
　目を覚すと、母がいた。私は安心して、ますます声を上げて泣いた。

Chapter 1

I was probably four or five years old. I was with my mother in a white building. The interior was clean and bright like a hospital. The building was standing by itself on a large plot of land surrounded by a high wall. I was somehow familiar with the building, navigating the corridors effortlessly.

Suddenly, my mother took my hand and started walking. She left the building and headed to the entrance. When we reached the wall, she pushed me outside, closed the gate, and returned to the building. She didn't say anything.

Outside the gate, the world was dark. I was all alone. Terrified, I started screaming, calling out for my mother.

"Did you have a bad dream, again?"

Waking, I saw my mother's face. With relief, I cried even harder.

Chapter 2

　私のアゲハ・ラブは、紆余曲折の末に生まれた。薬草に興味を持って、鉢植えの小さな山椒の木を育て始めたのがきっかけだった。山椒の葉は、新陳代謝を促してくれるので、日々の食卓に乗せようと思ったのだ。

　ところが5月に旅行からもどってみると、イモ虫が数匹、大切な葉をむさぼり食っていた。焦げ茶に白がまじった、鳥のフンのような虫だった。気持ちが悪くなって、虫に触れないように虫がついた葉をむしりとると、下の草むらめがけてバルコニーから落とした。これで、事が済んだと思った。

　数日後、我が一族の昆虫博士なる8歳の甥にその話をした。すると「おばちゃん、それはアゲハの幼虫です。山椒とみかん科の木の葉しか食べません」という。なんか申し訳ない気がした。バルコニーから落としたあの虫たちは、草むらの中で、みな餓死したことになる。

　数日後、その気の緩みをつくように、山椒にまた1匹の幼虫がはいはじめた。おそらく、こいつだけを見落としてしまったにちがいない。唯一の生存虫を前に、自問自答してみる。

　「こんな汚らしいものが、本当にあの美しいアゲハになるのだろうか？ 子供の頃、夢中になって追いかけたアゲハだ。一宿一飯の恩義がある……のではないか」

　仕方なく植木鉢をバルコニーの端に置いて、遠目に見ることにした。

　心のどこかで、茶と白が混ざったイモ虫が、美しい蝶になる瞬間を期待して待っていると、3日後、アゲハどころか、緑色の肉質なイモムシに変わってしまった。しかも、白黒の斑点まである。もう限界だ。

　翌日、マクベス夫人のように夫の行動を待つことなどはせず、自らが、殺虫剤を片手に木に近づいていった。木は、ほぼまる裸になっていた。それに、幼虫の姿が見えない。

　「しめしめ、無血革命か……」

　一瞬、期待が心をかすめたが、何気に視線を落とせば、幼虫が植

Chapter 2

My fascination with swallowtails was not voluntary. I was actually interested in medicinal herbs. I had been cultivating a small pot of prickly ash for its metabolic properties. This plant was going to contribute to our daily meals.

Returning from a trip in May, I was shocked to find my precious plant invaded by small brown and white striped worms. These bugs, which looked like bird droppings, were dining on my leaves. I was disgusted. To avoid touching the things, I pinched off each leaf occupied by a bug and hurled it into the field below the balcony. Having saved my prickly ash from these foreign invaders, I thought little of it—at least until a conversation with the family entomologist.

My eight-year-old nephew knows everything about bugs. He told me that these worms were actually the caterpillar of the swallowtail butterfly. He explained they only eat the leaves of two types of plants: prickly ash and citrus trees. Suddenly, I felt guilty; did I doom these creatures to starvation when I threw them into the field?

As fate would have it, a few days later, I found a solitary swallowtail caterpillar on a leaf. I must have missed this one when I banished the others. Presented with this survivor, I hesitated. Can this ugly creature really transform into those beautiful swallowtails I chased as a child? How can I kill something that brought me such joy? Not knowing what to do, I put the pot in the corner of my balcony and watched.

For three days, I observed my plant with the expectation that this small, white and brown bug would turn into a magnificent swallowtail. I was not ready for what came next. This small bug was replaced with a larger one: a fleshy bright-green caterpillar covered in black and white spots.

The next day, like Lady Macbeth not waiting for her husband to act, I approached it with a bottle of pesticide. The prickly ash was desolate, having lost most of its leaves.

　木鉢の横でぐったりとしていた。お腹が空いて、他にも食べられる葉はないものかと探しに出たが、力尽きたのだろう。
　さっきまで持っていた殺意は、一体、どこへ行ったのやら。あわてて山椒の木に残っていた最後の一葉をとり、口へ持っていった。小指の先よりも小さな葉だったが、幼虫は生き返ったように上半身を上げた。小さく細い前足で、ハッシとばかりに葉をつかむと、無我夢中で食べはじめた。
　「前足が6本もある……のか」
　あまりにしっかりとつかんでいるので、引いてみたい衝動にかられたが、幼虫はあっという間に非常食を完食してしまった。そして、どこが目だかはわからないが、心なしに物言いたげな角度で私と対峙した。
　「まだ欲しいのか？　おまえ、そんなに生きたいのか」
　情に溺れるとは、このことか……、幼虫をとりあえず木にもどそうと、自分の人差し指を提供してしまったと気がついたときには、すでに遅かった。幼虫は頭を小刻に振って、指に前足をかけた。すると突然、いきなり無数とも見える後足が、ニョキニョキと動きはじめた。恐れおののいて指を引いたら、今度は2.5cmぐらいしかなかったはずの体が、アコーディオンのように伸びた。同時に、緑のからだの側面に走っていた小さな白黒の点々も、にゅ～と大きく横に伸びた。これにより、こちらの体はフリーズ。目だけが、おかまいなしに指に乗ってくる幼虫を追った。
　すると、不思議な事が起きた。自分の本能的な反応が、実際に経験している事と合わなくなってきたのだ。目は、狂ったように拒絶信号を送ってくるのに、指からの感触がなんて優しいのだろう……。幼虫は、噛みつくこともない。チクチクと刺すこともない。殺人未遂犯に全身をゆだね、ブニョブニョとゆっくり歩みを進めてくるではないか。
　「あまりに無防備すぎる。こんなものが、この世に生かされているなんて、むごすぎる……」
　幼虫を植木鉢の裸の木にもどすと、自転車に飛び乗り園芸店を目指した。

I peered in, but the invader was gone. I couldn't find it. *Thank god*, I thought; this was going to be a bloodless revolution.

My relief soon vanished as I spotted the caterpillar lying exhausted and starved next to the pot. It must have left the plant to look for food, using up its strength in the attempt.

My murderous intent suddenly dissolved. I hastily plucked the last leaf from the prickly ash and offered it to the caterpillar. The leaf was smaller than the tip of my little finger. The caterpillar raised its body, grabbed the leaf, and began to eat. I could see six tiny legs firmly holding the leaf. I resisted the urge to pull back and deny the creature its prize. The caterpillar finished the emergency food. It seemed to gaze at me with anticipation (although I had no idea where its eyes were).

"Do you want some more? You really want to live, don't you?"

Completely lost in the moment, I reached out to put it back on the plant. The caterpillar appeared to sniff my finger and then lifted itself, touching me with its myriad legs. I recoiled at the sight, stretching its one-inch body like an accordion: the small black and white spots on its sides flexed with it. I froze as the caterpillar marched nonchalantly onto my finger.

The dissonance between my instinct and my experience overwhelmed me: my mind was repulsed by this alien invader, but my heart was touched by its gentleness. The caterpillar didn't bite or sting. It casually walked up the finger of this former assassin, its soft, flabby body swaying left and right. Its defenselessness confused me even more; how can something like this survive in the world?

Once returning it to the safety of the prickly ash, I jumped on my bicycle and headed to the garden center.

Chapter 3

　理性とは、もろいものだ。気がついたときには、数センチしかない1匹のイモ虫のために、1ｍぐらいあるミカンの木を新調していた。その上、やはり気持ち悪さが抜けなかった。

　そんなある日、洗濯物を干していると、突然、小さな音が聞こえてきた。

　「カリカリ、カリカリ」

　気のせいだと思って干し続けると、また、

　「カリカリ、カリカリ」

　耳をすまして音の方向を探ると、ミカンの木の方からだ。

　「まさか他の虫まで住みついたのか？」

　仁王立ちして、木をにらんだ。が、皿のようになった目が捉えたものは、葉緑素たっぷりの緑色の葉をかじっている、あの幼虫の姿だった。葉の端を、また前足でしっかりとつかんでいる。夢中である。おいしそうである。

　「41年も生きてきたけど、聞いたことがない音っていうものが、この世にはまだまだあるんだなぁ」

　この音によって、幼虫は見事に「マイ・ペット」へと昇進した。

　それからは、毎日、幾度となくバルコニーに出て、幼虫の様子を見るようになった。無数に見えた後足も、たった10本と認識できるようになり、衣装については、カモフラージュのためにミカンの木を真似たにちがいないと、賞賛の対象となった。

　しかし、今度はあちらが、私の姿に動きを止めるはめになった。食事中に不意打ちを食らわすと、意地汚くも葉を口にくわえたまま、じっとしていることもあった。

　ときには上半身を思いっきり起こしたまま、静止するはめに陥っ

Chapter 3

Why is reason so vacillating? I bought a three-foot orange tree for an animal barely an inch long. And yet, this insect still repelled me.

One day, hanging laundry, I heard strange, faint sound:
Kari-kari-kari…

I shrugged it off and continued to hang laundry.
Kari-kari-kari…

I stopped and listened. It was emanating from the orange tree. (I hoped it was not another bug!)

I peered into the tree. But instead of finding a new insect invader, I saw the caterpillar munching on a mature green leaf. It held this meal tightly between its front feet, devouring it with relish.

After 41 years of life, I was amazed that I could still discover new sounds. With this one melody, the caterpillar, *my* caterpillar, was promoted to an official pet.

As the days went on, I often visited the balcony to check on it. I soon became familiar with my new friend. I recognized that it only had ten legs, not the countless I imagined. As for its appearance, it earned my admiration as a clever camouflage for its host tree.

But our roles reversed. Instead of me freezing in the presence of this animal, I realized the caterpillar froze in mine. When I appeared in the middle of its dinner, it would became motionless—but still greedily holding onto its meal.

Sometimes, it raised its upper body, eventually freezing in that position. I began to test this response. I stood in front of the caterpillar and timed its ability to keep that posture. (I admit, I was also being a little mean.) Just as I expected, within a few minutes, the caterpillar's upper body started

ている。そんな姿勢で、どれぐらいじっとしていられるものか、意地悪にも横に立ってずっと見ていたら、案の定、数分のうちに上半身がだんだん前に傾いてきて、最後には「無念、これまで……」とばかりに、前に倒れこんだ。ところが、そのあとがいじらしい。「自分としたことが、なんたる失態！」と言わんばかりに、懲りもせずに無理な状態に姿勢をもどしたのである。

　ある晩、昆虫学者さながら、幼虫のこの生態観察の結果を夫に報告した。

　「虫だって、すべてが本能に支配されているわけじゃないのよ。意識的に、じっとしているのよ。生き残るために、がんばっているのよ」

　夫は、まじまじと私をみた。

　「イモ虫相手に、『ダルマさんが転んだ』か？」

leaning forward and eventually collapsed, as if to declare, *that's it, I'm done!* But, touchingly, it would suddenly recover as if embarrassed by its lapse of willpower.

One night, I reported this new-found behavior to my husband like an entomologist. "Even bugs are not entirely controlled by their instinct. I am sure the caterpillar was consciously posing, doing its best to survive."

He stared at me, "are you telling me that you played Red Light, Green Light with a caterpillar?"

Chapter 4

ある朝、幼虫がいなくなっていた。葉はたくさん残っているから、他の木に移動するわけがない。あわてて次から次へと植木鉢やプランターを動かして探せば、壁伝いに歩いているのを見つけた。

　ほっとして、木に移そうと指に乗せたまではよかったが、驚いたことに、別の虫になっていた。ゆっくりとした歩みが、この虫の神聖さだったのに、指に乗るのも速かったが、乗るや否や一気に手のひらまではい、腕にまで迫ってきた。からだを激しく伸縮させ、大きく波打ちながら暴走してくる。たかがイモ虫に、こんな緊迫感を感じるとは……。

　「月にでも、はっていってやる！」

　そう言っているかのような、一心不乱ぶりだった。

　木にもどしても、あっという間に植木鉢の端まで下りてきて、下のコンクリーに向けてポトリと身投げする。ケガをしなかったかと心配すれば、すぐに正気づいて、猪のごとくまた走りだす。それを捕まえてはもどし、また逃げられてはもどしを3、4回繰り返したのち、ついにあきらめてほっておいた。

　その後の消息がわかったのは、2日後である。バルコニーの隅に置いてあったちり取りに、神妙に「く」の字に体を曲げ、蛹になって張り付いていた。おかげでちり取りは使えなくなり、窓辺に置いて観察することにした。

　2週間後、見てみれば、蛹は二つに割れて空になっていた。

　「どこへ飛んでいったのやら。幸運が、いつまでも続くといいけれど」

　バルコニーに出て、空を見上げた。あのアゲハの「運命の輪」の一部を、自分が担うことができたという喜びを感じていた。顔がほくそ笑み、小踊りしたくなってきた。この自分も、一連の幸運の延長線上に生まれたからだろうか？　もっともその事実を知ったのは、このアゲハの誕生から遡ること5年前だった。

Chapter 4

One day, the caterpillar was gone. I didn't understand why it would leave since there were plenty of leaves on the tree. Panicking, I searched the balcony, moving the pots and planters one after another. Finally, I found it crawling along the balcony wall.

With great relief, I reached out with my finger. But the caterpillar seemed possessed. Unlike the adorable ambling gait that was the symbol of the creature's holiness, this incarnation was bewitched. Without hesitation, it mounted my finger, headed across my palm, and up my arm. This new urgency created a heaving wave-like motion through its expanding and contracting body. The desperate determination in this tiny bug shocked me, as if this new compulsion would take it to the moon.

I placed it back in the tree. It immediately rushed down, climbed over the edge of the pot, and fell to the concrete floor. I was worried it injured itself. Despite my concern, it started running like a bull. I caught it again and put it back in the tree, only for it to run away again. After three or four attempts, I left it to nature.

Two days later, I discovered its destination: the dustpan in the corner of the balcony. It was no longer a caterpillar, but a chrysalis, mysteriously bent like a dogleg. Now that I couldn't use the dustpan, I moved it next to the window to observe its next transformation.

Two weeks later, the exterior of the chrysalis was split down the middle and empty. I stepped onto the balcony and looked up into the sky. I was overcome with joy, realizing that I could play a part in this butterfly's fortunes. With a giggle, I felt the urge to dance. Perhaps this joy was due in part to my own existence that hinged on a series of chance events, a history I only became aware of five years earlier.

Chapter 5

アゲハを育てる前、夫と私は、東京の私の両親の家に同居をしていた。私にしてみれば、結婚前と変わらない単調な生活であり、晩には、両親とニュース番組を見るのが日課になっていた。

　毎年8月に入ると、終戦記念日の15日にかけて、戦争関連のテレビ番組が続く。両親から、特攻隊や憲兵の怖さ、食糧難など、戦争中のひどい話を聞いてはいたが、両親の家族の中に、出兵どころか空襲を受けたり、戦死した人がいなかったせいか、戦争番組を対岸の火事のような感覚でいつも見ていた。

　その年の夏の8月9日の晩も同様で、夫の帰宅を待ちながら、午前中に長崎の平和公園で行われた平和式典の様子をテレビで見ていた。長崎の平和公園も、姉が結婚する前に家族で行ったので、家族旅行の思い出の場所にすぎなかった。ただ、両親は長崎と同じ九州の鹿児島で育ったので、その晩、なんてことなしに聞いた。

　「長崎に原爆が落ちた時、こんな酷いものが落ちたことなんて知っていた？」

　「知らない、知らない。ただの爆弾だと思ったよ」

　父が、大きく手を振って答えた。母は、黙っている。

　「そうだよね。知っているわけがないよね。二人とも子供だったし、鹿児島の家にいたんだもんね」

　質問したつもりはなかったが、母を見ればうなずいたので、ついでに父の方も見れば、

　「長崎にいた」

　ぼそっと言った。聞きまちがえたと思って、

　「この時だよ？」

　テレビ画面を指しながら聞きなおすと、父は、へなへな笑ってうなずいた。何をバカな冗談を言っているのか。

　「原爆が落ちた当日のことを聞いてるの」と繰り返せば、

　「だから、あそこにいたって」

Chapter 5

Before raising swallowtails, my husband and I lived with my parents in Tokyo. Life was pretty routine in my family. Every evening, we sat together to watch the news.

Every August, annual commemorations marking the end of the Second World War are held. Between August 1st and 15th, documentaries related to the war are broadcast. I, like in previous years, had watched them like a fire on the other side of the river, that is, with indifference. My parents had told me some terrible stories from the war: suicide attacks by the Japanese air force, the brutality of the military police, and shortages of food. However, nobody in their families were sent to the front, bombed, or killed, which probably led to my apathy.

This particular August 9th was no different as I watched the evening news with my parents while waiting for my husband to return home. A ceremony commemorating the dropping of the atomic bomb on Nagasaki, held in the Peace Memorial Park that morning, was on TV. The only connection I had to Nagasaki was a family trip taken before of my sister's marriage.

I knew my parents had grown up on the same island of Kyushu during the war. I casually asked, "when the atomic bomb hit Nagasaki, did you know that it was such a terrible weapon?"

My father said, shaking his hand with uncharacteristic vigor, "no, no, I thought that it was just an another bomb."

My mother was silent.

"Of course, you couldn't have known that. You two were still children and living with your parents in Kagoshima, weren't you?"

It was not really a question, but my mother nodded in agreement. I looked at my father.

"I was in Nagasaki," he mumbled.

声が鋭くなっている。

父の手からあわててリモコンを奪うと、テレビの音量を落とした。

「あそこって、どこよ」

私の声もきつくなったてきた。

「だから、長崎市内」

父は苦い顔をし、母を見れば、半ばあきらめの表情を浮かべている。

「市内の……どこよ」

私の声がかすれた。父は頭の後ろをかきはじめ、しでかしたドジを白状する少年のように言った。

「青年学校[1]に通っていたんだ。今で言えば中学校か。原爆が投下された場所のすぐそばにあったはずだ」

市内の中学校？ どういうこと？ そんなはずがない……。この人が、そんな経験をしているはずがない。

訳もない反発が、体中に湧いてきた。14年前に長崎旅行をしたとき、平和記念像の前で家族の記念写真まで撮った。浦上天主堂とかも、観光してまわった。あのとき、父は何も言わなかった。思い出にふける素振り一つ、見せなかった。それなのに、今になっていきなり何を言い出すのか。

父をめがけて、ぶっきらぼうな言葉が飛び出した。

「なんで生きているのよ」

I must have heard him wrong. "I mean, on that day?" pointing at the TV screen.

He nodded with a sheepish smile. I thought he must have been kidding.

"I mean, the day the atomic bomb was dropped," I repeated.

His voice became shaper. "I told you. I was there."

I snatched the TV remote out of his hand and lowered the volume. "Where? In Nagasaki?" My voice was now strained, too.

"I told you, in Nagasaki city." He frowned. I saw a resigned look on my mother's face.

"Exactly where…in Nagasaki city?" My voice cracked.

He started scratching his head like a boy about to confess a transgression.

"I was a student in a junior high school, called a Youth School[1] then, in the city. It was near where the bomb hit."

What did he mean by *a junior high school in the city*? What is he talking about? It can't be true. It is impossible that he, this human being, had such an experience. I couldn't grasp what I was hearing. A wave of anger suddenly came over me. On a trip to Nagasaki 14 years before, we took family photos in front of the Peace Statue. We went to the Urakami Cathedral. We walked around the city. Yet, he didn't say anything. He didn't show any sign of recognition then. Why now? Why did he tell me now? My next question was blunt.

"Why are you alive!"

Chapter 6

1945年の春、14歳の少年は予科練²の試験を受けようと村を出た。空軍に入って、敵機をかたっぱしから撃ち落としてやる計画だった。

　ところが、予想外の事が起きた。途中で目の感染症にかかってしまい、健康診断で試験に落ちてしまったのだ。お国の役にたたない人間は「非国民」であり、とくに男は少年であろうが、大人であろうが、家の恥。隣人どころか、家族に会わせる顔もない。思いつめた少年は、かつて人づてに聞いたことがある長崎の青年学校へ向かった。

　そして、無事に入学を果たすと、学生寮にも入れてもらい、毎朝寮から級友らと共に、歩いて学校へ通学することになった。

　ある夏の朝も、いつものように学校へ行った。ところが急に頭痛が始まり、頭が割れるようでどうにも耐えられない。

　「先生、頭痛がひどいので早退させてください」

　少年にとっては初めてのことだったし、校則や教師たちは厳しかった。が、意外にも簡単に許可され、ひとり学校を出て寮へ向かった。

　すると、上級生がどこからともなく現れて、後をつけてきた。少年が小さな店の前を通り過ぎようとすると、急に追いついてきて命令した。

　「かき氷をおごれ」

　少年は言われるままに店に入って、かき氷をおごると、また寮へと向かった。

　寮の玄関のドアを開けて中に入ると、

　「きさま、な、な、なにものだー」

　寮長が、悲鳴をあげた。顔面蒼白になって、後ずさりしていく。

　「寮長、大坪であります」

Chapter 6

In spring 1945, this 14 year-old boy made up his mind:
he would leave home and join the Japanese Naval Aviation
Preparatory School.[2] He had an image of entering the air
force and shooting down every enemy plane to protect his
country.

On his journey, he unexpectedly contracted an
eye infection. This resulted in him failing the physical
examination. This failure to serve his country not only
brought him shame, but also his family. He could not return
home after this. He heard that there was a Youth School in
Nagasaki. He would go there.

He enrolled in the school and was given housing in a
nearby dormitory. Every day, he and his classmates would
make the journey between the dormitory and school.

One summer morning, he went to class as usual. While
sitting in class, he noticed a headache coming on. In a
few minutes, it became unbearable. He raised his hand,
"teacher, I have a terrible headache. I would like to go
back to the dormitory." The boy had never done this
before; the school was strict about attendance and the
boy was always mindful of the rules. To his surprise, his
request was granted.

On his way back to the dormitory, he noticed one of the
senior students following him. When the boy was passing a
small store along the route, the senior caught up with him.
The command was abrupt, "hey, kid, buy me some shaved
ice." The boy obeyed and they entered the store.

After eating the shaved ice, he continued on his way to
the dormitory. He opened the entrance and stepped into the
hallway.

「そ、そんなはずがない。幽霊だろう」
「ちがいます。自分は、学校を早退したのであります」
「嘘をつけ」
「本当であります」
「脚をあるか？ 脚をみせろ、脚を」
　寮長は、少年の脚を血走った目でよくよく見ると、腰が抜けたようにヘタヘタとその場に座りこんでしまった。無理もない。その日の午後、少年の級友は、だれも戻ってはこなかった。

The house master appeared. "Who…who…who the devil are you?" he screamed. Visibly pale, the house master stepped back.

"I am Otsubo, master."

"You are lying. You can't be him. Are you a ghost?"

"No, sir. I left school early."

"Do you have legs? Show me your legs!"[3]

The house master stared with blood-shot eyes at the boy's legs. Suddenly, he collapsed with relief. No one else in the boy's class would return to the dormitory that day.

Chapter 7

父の話は、信じがたいものだった。宝くじ一つ当てたことがないし、路上で宗教団体の人が、「神が、あなたの問題を解決します。神に頼りなさい」と勧誘してくれば、「あんたは、かわいそうだ。自分の問題も、自分で解決できないのかね」と、平気で言って返すような人なのだ。傍目から見れば、幸運や神の奇跡から程遠い、ただ日々を淡々と生きる凡夫なのだ。そんな人間が、こんな命拾いをしていたとは……。

「つまり、頭痛のおかげで、死ななかったわけ？」

唖然として聞けば、父は、頭の後ろをかきながらうなずいた。父が置かれた状況をもっと知ろうと、

「その先輩は？」と聞けば、

「知らないよ」

肩をすくめて、彼のことは問題外という顔をした。

「被爆は？」

いきなり低い声で、切り込んだ。その唐突さと無神経さに、自分自身が驚いた。が、原爆と聞けば、これしかない。

「してない、してない」

父は、からだを震わせんばかりに、子供のように否定した。そんな父を斜めに見て、

「検査はした？」

「したよ、した」

二度も肯定すると、かえって怪しい。

「いったいどんな検査よ？」

ついに、取り調べモードになった。

「血液とか……　大丈夫だった。原爆が落ちた時、室内にいたからな。寮は山にあって、店はその山をまわりこんだところにあったんだ」

高圧的な口調になっていく私を落ち着かせようと、父は余裕をと

Chapter 7

I just couldn't believe my father's story. He was not born under a lucky star, never winning the lottery. If a religious person approached him on the street, saying, "god will solve your problems. Rely on god," he would respond, "can't you solve your own problems? I pity you." That is my father, a pragmatic man who lives day to day, not relying on fortune or gods. How could I imagine that this man had such a narrow escape?

I was dumbfounded. "So, you mean, you did not die because of a headache?"

He nodded, scratching the back of his head again.

"What happened to the senior?" I asked trying to understand the situation.

"No idea." He shrugged his shoulders with indifference.

With a low voice, I cut to the heart of the matter, "were you irradiated?" I was surprised at my abrupt, insensitive question, but there was nothing more important than this.

"No, no," he asserted, squirming like a child.

Giving him a sidelong glance, I continued,

"Did you have a medical examination?"

"I did, I did."

This double confirmation made me more suspicious. "What kind of tests did you have?" This conversation was turning into an interrogation.

"Well, for example, blood tests. I was fine. When the bomb exploded, I was inside a store and the store was behind the mountain where the school dormitory was."

In contrast to the increasing intensity of my voice, his answers were almost jocular, as if to wave away the irrational fear of a child. But it did not stop me from asking the most important question.

"Do you have an atomic-bomb victim record book?" If my father had been in the city, he would have an atomic-

りもどして笑った。しかし私は、おかまいなしに問いつめた。
　「被爆者手帳は？」
　問題は、これだ。父よ、あなたは、これを持っているのか？
　「持ってないよ。山は、爆心地帯っていわれる2キロ圏内からは、外れていたからな。圏外にいたんだよ」
　私は、ぽか～んとして父を見た。「圏外」という言葉が、私の中の不安をいきなり一括消去してしまい、何を質問していいのかわからなくなってしまった。
　話ができすぎている……そう疑う一方で、本当かもしれない……とも思えてきた。なぜなら、おしゃべりな母が、全く口をはさまない。ずっと黙って聞いている。彼女は、前々からこの話を知っていたのだ。この親は二人して、こんな大事なことを、娘に37年間も隠してきたのか？
　ともかく落ち着いて、頭を整理しなければいけない。つまり私が今日あるのは、父のひどい頭痛と、意地悪な上級生と、店と寮のロケーションのおかげということになるのか？
　父を見れば、身動き一つせず、こちらの出方を待っていた。
　「本当に、ラッキーだったね……」
　なんとかため息混じりに言えば、
　「ああ」
　父は照れ笑いを浮かべ、言葉になっていない返答をして口をつぐんだ。
　「どうして今まで黙っていたの？」
　簡単な質問でないことは、わかっていた。
　「そうか？　言わなかったか？」
　父もとぼけて、また頭をかいた。

bomb victim record book issued to survivors: this could be official proof that he was irradiated.

"No. The mountain where the store was located was outside the two-kilometer blast radius."

I was speechless. I stared at my father. His words *outside the two-kilometer blast radius* erased all the questions I was struggling to articulate.

His story sounded too implausible to be true. But could it be true? My mother, a naturally talkative woman, kept her silence. She must have known this. How could my parents, these two human beings, have been able to hide such a secret from their own daughter for 37 years?

I needed to calm down and organize my thoughts. I am here thanks to an unbearable headache, a school bully, and the random locations of a store and dormitory?

I looked at my father. He was calm, waiting for me to respond.

"I am happy for you, father. You were very lucky." I let out a deep breath.

"Yes…yes." He gave me an inexpressible answer with an embarrassed smile. That was all.

"Why didn't you tell me before?"

I knew this was not a simple question.

"Really, haven't I told you before?"

He scratched his head again, feigning innocence.

Chapter 8

最初の気まぐれな幼虫に、大豪邸を発作的に与えてしまったが、それに気がついたのは私だけではなかった。毎日のように、ヒラヒラとアゲハがやってくるようになった。せちがらい都会で、やっと卵を産みつけることができる貴重な木を見つけたのだ。見逃すはずがなかった。

　気がつけば、10匹ぐらいの幼虫がはいだし、みんな成長速度が同じだから、あっという間に葉を食べ尽くしてしまった。仕方なく、2本目を買った。それをまた別なアゲハが見つけて卵を生んだので、3本目を追加。

　こんな調子で6本目に達したとき、めったにバルコニーに出ない夫も気がついた。ひとりバルコニーに出て、虫の数を数えはじめたと思ったら、数分後に目を丸くして戻ってきた。

　「16匹もいる……。幼虫に、家賃を払ってもらえ！」

　実は、24匹もいた。おそらく8匹は葉の裏でじっとしていたので、目が慣れていない夫には、わからなかったのだろう。

　この後も、色々なミカン科の木がバルコニーいっぱいに並んでいき、数ヶ月のうちには12本になった。

　幼虫は、どんなに数が増えて混雑してきても、争うことなどしない。まるで、草原の羊のようだ。正面から出くわすと、おじぎこそしないものの、互いに道を譲りあうようにすれちがう。私にとっては、天国さながらの風景となった。

　いつの間にか、成長していくアゲハ・メトロポリスの写真まで撮るようになった。鳥のフンのようなものが、どうしてゴージャスなアゲハになるのか？ 進化の結果とはいえ、生まれ出たときには、似ても似つかない姿をしていたことを、アゲハたちは覚えているのだろうか。

Chapter 8

After impulsively providing an overly generous habitat for my wayward swallowtail, others noticed. Each day, a new swallowtail found the tree. In a hostile world, this was a rare sanctuary to lay eggs, an opportunity too good not to miss.

Before long, ten caterpillars had taken up residence. This brood of siblings grew together. They seemed to devour the foliage of this solitary tree in the blink of an eye. Reluctantly, I bought another. More swallowtails came and laid their eggs. I bought a third.

One day, my husband, who rarely went out to the balcony, realized something was up when I bought the sixth tree. After spending a few minutes alone on the balcony, he came back inside stunned. "I can't believe it. There are sixteen caterpillars out there. We should charge rent!" Actually, there were 24. He was not used to spotting them and missed eight, which were probably hiding on the back of the leaves.

Within a few months, my small balcony was full. My butterfly nursery comprised of a collection of twelve citrus trees of different varieties.

Even with this population growth, my caterpillars were never aggressive with each other. They are like sheep in pastures. When they do bump into each other, they don't bow like humans, but yield as if to say, *after you*. This peaceful community had become a vision of heaven for me.

I started photographing this growing swallowtail metropolis. How could something resembling bird poop become a glorious butterfly? It's a mystery. Although this life cycle is the result of evolution, I wondered if butterflies know they bear little resemblance to their previous incarnations?

Chapter 9

中学校の時、自分の家が元大名家であることを自慢にしていた先生がいた。社会科を教えていることをいいことに、家紋や先祖に関する宿題を出し、とにかく生徒の家柄を知りたがった。

　ある時その先生が、赤ん坊の時の写真を持ってくるように言った。しかも、生後間もないものでなければいけなかった。ところが自分のアルバムを見て、そんな写真がないことに初めて気がついた。一番古い写真は、生後１年ぐらいのもので、母の両腕に抱かれ、スカートもはいているし、靴もはいている。髪の毛も生えている。

　「私が生まれたときの写真は、どこにあるの？」と母に聞けば、別の部屋から、１枚のかわいい赤ん坊の写真をもってきた。大きな目をして髪の毛も薄く、ベビー服を着て布団の上をハイハイしている。「我ながら、かわいい……」と、それをもって学校に行った。

　20代になったときだった。久しぶりにアルバムの整理をしていると、姉がアルバムの一つを手に取って見始めたと思ったら、あの赤ん坊の写真を指して、首をかしげた。

　「なんで私の赤ん坊の写真が、ここに入っているの？」

　父母は、私が生まれたとき、一枚も写真を撮らなかったのだ。私には、生まれたときの写真がない。どんな顔をしてこの世に出てきたのか、知ることができない。そんな親が、いるのだろうか？　母子手帳の記載や父親似の外見から、私が養子でないことは確かだ。しかも、姉の赤ん坊の時の写真はたくさんある。

　悲しい怒りを覚えて母に詰め寄れば、

　「お父さんが、男の子をほしがっていたの。でも、女の子が生まれたから、がっかりして撮らなかったのよ」

　聞くんじゃなかった。予想外に、ひどい答えだ。父は、姉が生まれ

Chapter 9

At junior high school, I had a social science teacher who was very proud of his family heritage, often talking about his ancestors that served as a feudal lord to a Shogun. He also took a keen interest in his student's family backgrounds, often assigning them to collect information on their ancestral history.

One day, he asked us to bring in baby photos taken right after our birth. Going through my childhood photographs, I realized that my earliest picture was taken when I was around one. The image was of me wearing a skirt and shoes and being held by my mother. I had hair.

I asked my mother where the photos of when I was born were. She brought out a cute baby photo from another room. The picture showed an infant with thin hair and big eyes, crawling on a bed in a baby suit. I was struck by how sweet I looked. I took it to school.

In my 20s, I decided to organize my photo albums. My sister was flipping through one of the albums and stopped. She pointed at the cute baby photo. Puzzled, she asked, "why is my baby photo here?"

It suddenly dawned on me: my parents never took a photo of me when I was born. I have no record of how I looked when I came into this world. Why would they not do that? What parents don't photograph their babies? My birth certificate and resemblance to my father are evidence I am not adopted. What made this worse was they took a plenty of photos of my sister when she was born.

Being sad and angry, I confronted my mother.

"Your father wanted a boy very badly, but you turned out to be a girl. He was disappointed."

たときはうれしくて、毎日のようにチョコレートを買って与えようとして、医者に叱られたと聞いている。男の子が欲しかっただと？ ふざけるな。開いた口がふさがらなくなり、怒る気もしなくなった。この時ほど、父が他人に思えたことはなかった。

　ところが10年後、アメリカの義母が、くすぶっていた私の悲しみと怒りを呼び起こしてしまった。私に、めちゃくちゃ可愛い夫のベビー写真をくれたのだ。赤ん坊は、ふわふわのベビーブランケットに包まれて、天上のお花畑でも見ているかのような無邪気な笑顔を浮かべていた。
　私はまたもや、母を責めた。
　「理由がどうであれ、1年もの間、写真を1枚も撮らなかったのはひどすぎるじゃない。お母さんだって、写真が撮れたはずよ。恥ずかしくて、人にも言えないわよ」
　母は、申し訳なさそうにしゅんとしてしまい、やっと重い口を開いた。
　「実は、あなたは生まれたとき、『アーアー』と3回ぐらいしか泣かなかったし、白目が多くて、医者から『目が見えないかもしれない』と言われたのよ。フラッシュをたいて写真を撮ることを、しばらく禁じられていたの」
　まあ、これなら前の言い訳よりは、もっともらしい。医者の命令となれば、やむを得まい……。最初から、そう言ってくれればいいものを。以来、私はこの件をすっかり忘れてしまった。

　けれど、幼虫の写真を撮りはじめてから、死んだふりをしていた不満がまた復活しはじめた。写真を撮るということは、人生の幸せな瞬間を記録に残したいという気持ちに他ならない。私の親は、私の誕生に対して、そんな感情を持たなかったのだろうか？ 二人して1年もの間、何をしていたのだろう。

I shouldn't have asked; this was a much worse explanation than I expected. When my sister was born, my father was overjoyed and bought her chocolate every day—a habit that was stopped by her doctor.

He wanted a boy! What the hell? I was too disgusted to confront him. My father seemed like a total stranger to me.

Ten years later, my American mother-in-law reawakened my suppressed sadness and anger. She gave me an extremely cute baby photo of my husband. He was gently wrapped in a soft, baby blanket, smiling happily as if he was looking up at a flower garden in heaven.

I confronted my mother again. "Whatever the reason, I just can't believe that you two didn't take any photos of me for a whole year after my birth! Mom, you could have taken my photo if you wanted to. I can't tell my friends; it is just too embarrassing."

Chest fallen, my mother confessed. "To tell you the truth, when you were born, you were so weak and could barely cry. Your eyes were so white that our doctor warned us that you might be blind and ordered us not to take photos with a flash for a while."

This story was more convincing—doctor's orders. Who could argue with that? But she could have told me in the beginning. I never raised the issue again.

Photographing my caterpillars years later reminded me of this. Taking pictures is an act of capturing and keeping happy moments in our lives. I wonder if my parents didn't think of my birth as a happy moment for them? What was happening in that year after I was born?

Chapter 10

最初の幼虫と同じように、その後の幼虫も丸々太ってくると、態度が豹変した。ゆったりとした歩みが、この虫の神聖さだったのに、一度その動きが始まると、道をふさぐ仲間のおしりを頭でこづいてどかせた。蛹があれば、おかまいなしにその上をはっていった。蛹の糸が切れて蛹が落ちても、かまうものか。「急げ、急げ、急げー、安全なところを探せ」とばかり、警報に怯えるかように無我夢中で、数時間動きまわった。

　それもそのはずで、この動きに入る前に、大量の尿とフンの混合物を排出しているから、いつまでも探し続けるエネルギーがない。つまり力尽きた所が、運の尽き場だった。

　たいていは、植木鉢の裏や壁と棚の間など、ミカンの木に近くて人目につかない所を選んで蛹となっていたので、この幼虫の豹変は、限られた時間内にできるだけ安全な場所を探すという本能的な行動だと、私にもわかってきた。

　実際、よく見てみれば、まわりには天敵がたくさんいた。ツバメが飛びまわり、ハトはアパートの屋上で群れている。近くの木では、子ガラス２羽が、母ガラスの両方について、羽をバタバタさせて餌をねだる。しかし、私の小さなバルコニーは、安全だと思っていた。

　そんな脳天気な私の頭にショック電流が流れたのは、7月になってからだった。植木棚の下で、何かが小さく動いているのが目に入った。近よってみれば、３cmぐらいの蛹が、からだをクネクネと動かしている。蛹になると、羽化するまでの２週間は全く動かないものだと思っていたので、身震いするほど仰天した。顔を近づけてみれば、３mmぐらいの小さな黒いハチが、蛹にとまっていた。蛹は、腹筋を使って体を激しく揺らし、必死にハチを振り払おうとしていたのだった。

　調べたところ、この不届き者はアオムシコバチというもので、こいつにやられた蛹は羽化できない。必死で見つけた秘密の場所で、ハチの幼虫なんぞに内からむさぼり食われて死ぬ。最後に残るのは、

Chapter 10

Just like with my first caterpillar, when my new brood became really fat, their peaceful natures changed. They hastily pushed past slower caterpillars, ramming them with their heads and forcing them aside. If there was a chrysalis in their way, they crawled over it without hesitation, sometimes cutting the silk anchoring the chrysalis, causing it to fall. They are single minded—*hurry, hurry, hurry, got to find a safe place!*—dashing around for a few hours as if reacting to a siren.

Before entering this panic, they rid themselves of their last meal, a mixture of pee and poop, which sets the timer for finding refuge. When they run out of that frantic energy, the place they find themselves can seal their fate.

Most of my caterpillars brilliantly choose hidden areas close to their host orange tree: the back of pots or the space between the wall and shelving. Seeing the places they chose to be chrysalis, I realized that their sudden change in behavior is instinctive and solely focused on finding the safest place possible in a limited time.

When I looked out from the balcony, I saw their natural enemies surrounding them—swallows patrolled the sky and pigeons perched on roofs. In a tree near my window, two fledgling crows flapped their wings, begging their mother for food. Nevertheless, I felt my small balcony was safe from any danger.

July was when nature shocked me from my innocence. I saw something moving under the shelves of the citrus trees. A small three centimeter chrysalis was twisting its body. I was stunned because I thought chrysalises couldn't move for the two weeks before they emerged. I took a closer look. A small three millimeter fly was on the chrysalis. The chrysalis was trying in vain to shake the fly off, limited by the motion of its abdominal muscles.

黒ずんだ蛹だけ。しかも、横に穴が空いている。この現実を知ってから、蛹になってからの「動けない2週間」という時間が、どれだけ恐怖に満ちたものか、私にもわかってきた。

そこで、木に大きな洗濯ネットをかけ、下をひもで縛って、蛹や幼虫の安全を確保することにした。あとは、蛹が羽化して蝶になる寸前に、ネットをとってあげればいい。自分にも、なかなか智恵がついてきたと思った。

According to my research, this villain has a name: *ptermalus puparum*. A chrysalis cannot survive an attack from this predator. In the secret hiding place where the swallowtail hangs after its hard labor, this tiny fly can end its journey, leaving only a blackened shell with a hole in its side. It was a chilling thought to hang defenseless for two weeks.

I made a plan: I would put laundry nets over the trees and tie them at the bottom to secure the safety of my swallowtails. When they are about to emerge as a butterfly, I will open the net and let them out. I am getting smarter. I smiled.

Chapter 11

　私の自負は、早々に打ち砕かれてしまった。ある日、ネットの下の方で1匹が蛹になってしまい、ネットをひもで縛りにくくなったので、ひもを少しだけ緩めておいたら、その日の夕方にはその蛹が消えてしまった。蛹を支えていた糸だけが、虚しく風に揺れていた。

　「蛹は、はって動けるのか……？」

　小学生でさえ持たないような愚かな疑問が、夜の間も頭から離れず、翌朝に早起きしてカーテンを開けてみれば、1羽の雀がネットの中にいた。なんと、幼虫をくわえていた。

　雀は、私を見た。ボトッと、獲物を落とした。ここまでは、コソ泥らしいあわてようだった。しかし、次の瞬間にフワァと舞い上がると、美しいJの字を余裕で描いて急降下し、ネットと植木鉢のわずかな隙間から出ていった。無駄のないみごとな動きで、羽をばたつかせもしなかった。

　「あばよ！」

　眼が合った瞬間、やつはそう言ったな。

　我に返って幼虫の数を数えてみれば、6匹もいない。あの鳥は昨夜も、蛹だけでなく幼虫も食べたのだ。口にくわえて枝に打ち付け、失神させて食らったにちがいない。

　なぜあの雀には、私がネットの縛りを緩めたのがわかったのか？外側からは、見えないはずだ。しかも緩めたのは、ネットを設置したこの1ヶ月の間で初めてだった。それを、あの雀は見のがさなかった。どおりで幼虫が、蛹になる安全な場所を一心不乱になって探すわけだ。

　どこで蛹になるか……？ それは本当に生死をわける問題で、しかも、どの幼虫も直面しなければならない。生き残るのは、100個の卵のうち、せいぜい1個だという。1頭のアゲハが100から300の卵を生むから、種の存続としては十分なのだろう。でも、1匹1匹の幼虫レベルでみれば、恐怖にみちた虫生だ。

Chapter 11

My victory was short lived. One day, I found a chrysalis
at the bottom of the net, making it difficult to tie up. I
loosened the strings so as to give the chrysalis a little space.
By the evening of the same day, the chrysalis was gone. Only
the silk thread supporting its body was left swinging in the
wind.

"Can chrysalises move?" This question, which wouldn't
have crossed the mind of an elementary school student,
stayed with me all night. The next morning, I woke up earlier
than usual. I opened the curtain. A sparrow had gotten into
the net. And it had *my* chrysalis in its beak!

The sparrow looked at me and dropped its prey like a
thief caught in its crime. But in the next moment, the bird
leaped effortlessly into the air and dived, drawing a beautiful
J through space as it escaped through the narrow gap
between the net and pot. It was a well calculated and graceful
execution, without a single ruffled feather. Instead, it gave a
simple *ciao* as our eyes met.

Recovering myself, I counted the remaining residents
in the tree. Six caterpillars were missing, along with the
chrysalis. Last evening, the bird must have had quite a feast.
Holding its prey in its beak, it would beaten them against the
tree to stun them before eating them.

How did the sparrow know that I loosened the net? I
thought I did it in such a way that it wouldn't be detected
from the outside. And that was the first time the net was
open for over a month since I had been using it. But the bird
didn't miss the opportunity. No wonder these caterpillars run
so desperately before they become chrysalises.

Choosing where to turn into a chrysalis is a matter of
life and death. Every one of them has to go through this
process. Only one out of every 100 eggs survives to become
a butterfly. Not great odds, but it is probably enough to

　ネットの中では、命拾いした幼虫たちが、葉にしがみついて死んだように動かなかった。仲間があの雀に食べられている間も、こうしてじっとしていたにちがいない。

　天敵がいる生物にとっては、これが生き残るということなのか。計り知れないほどの深い恐怖が、種の保存のために記録され、子孫に伝わっていく。もちろん、生き残るための知恵もつくから、こうした経験を「学習」ということもできる。しかし、学習ならば、サド的なひどいカリキュラム設定だ。生物は、こんな方法でしか学べないのだろうか？

　おかげでこの後、ハイキングにいっても、癒しどころではなくなった。生き物に、ただただ恐怖を見るようになった。私を見て逃げない動物など、1匹もいないではないか。野鳥は飛び去り、リスは木に逃れ、鹿は警報の叫びをあげる。思えば、子供の頃に「あっ、チョウチョ！」とか言って、花に止まっていた蝶を何も考えないでつまんだり、虫かごに入れたりしたが、私の小さな指やあどけない行為の裏に潜んでいたものは、いったい何だったのか？　私は、彼らにとっては天敵なのだ。

preserve the species since every butterfly lays between 100
and 300 eggs. From an individual swallowtail's point of view,
it must be a terrifying existence.

Inside the net, the surviving caterpillars were frozen,
holding tightly to their leaves after the trauma of the
sparrow's raid. These souls must have been just as still now as
they were when the other caterpillars were being devoured.

Is this the meaning of survival for creatures that
have natural enemies? Immeasurable fear is imprinted
and transmitted to each generation for the sake of the
preservation of the species. You can call it learning, but what
a dreadful sadistic curriculum. Can there be another way for
living creatures to learn?

Since this event, I started seeing the fear in animals
everywhere. Hiking in nature is far from healing now. There
isn't a single wild creature which won't run from me. As soon
as I am spotted, birds fly away, squirrels climb trees, and
deer sound an alarm. In retrospect, during my childhood, I
plucked butterflies from the flowers without hesitation. What
thoughts lurked behind my tiny fingers and innocent face
then? They all think I will kill them...a natural enemy.

Chapter 12

「父は、あの日、どんな思いをしたのだろうか」

　この3年の間、蛹となる場所を求めて動き回る幼虫に、人間の姿を重ねるようになっていた。そして、自然と父へとつながっていった。父を沈黙させてきたものの正体を、もっと知りたい。

　初めて話を聞いて以来、長崎の話は全くしていない。あの後、私たち夫婦が引越したせいもあるが、両親が長い間沈黙してきたことを思うと、土足で踏み込むわけにはいかなかった。

　自分で調べるしかない。今までそうしなかったのが、不思議なぐらいだ。やはり自分も、真実を知ることが怖かったのかもしれない。18歳の夏に広島の平和記念資料館を訪ねたが、写真を見て、あまりの惨さに耐えきれず、トイレに駆け込んで吐いた。後にも先にも、そんな経験をしたことはなかったから、父の話を「なんて幸運な！」というレベルで、終わらせたいという気持ちがあった。しかし、それで終わるはずがない。幼虫を見れば、一目瞭然のことだった。

　まず、インターネットで当時の爆心地帯の地図をみつけ、そこから学校を探すことにした。父は、名前もはっきりと覚えていなかった。入学して3、4ケ月後に原爆が落ちて、すぐに郷里にもどったので、記憶らしい記憶がないらしい。病院が近くにあって、学校は三菱重工がやっていて、動員学徒[3]として入学したと言っていた。

　それに、学生寮があった山はどれだろう？　川を渡った……と言っていたが、どの川なのか？

　7年前に父から聞いた話を手がかりに、被爆体験者のリポートを読み始めた。すると、「原爆が500m上空で炸裂して、閃光がすべてを覆い隠した」という文が目にとまった。ハッとした。父から聞いた話は、おかしい。山の裏手にいたとしても、屋内にいたとしても、閃光に気がつかなかったはずがない。

　さらに、三菱重工に勤めていた人のレポートの中に、「原爆が落ちた日に、救援のための召集がかかった」と書かれてある。ということ

Chapter 12

How did my father feel on that day?

For three years, I have been superimposing images of my caterpillars racing for a safety onto human beings. This brought me to thoughts of my father. What had silenced him for so long?

Since the day he told his story, we haven't talked. After moving out of my parent's house, there hasn't been an opportunity. Partially, my hesitancy has been respect for my parent's privacy: they had kept this secret for such a long time for a reason.

One day, it dawned on me: why can't I do my own research? I was hesitant about digging into this history. At 18, I visited the Hiroshima Peace Memorial Museum. Looking at the photographs, I was traumatized by the unbelievable cruelty: I rushed into the museum bathroom at some point and vomited. I have never had such a visceral experience before or since. Maybe I wanted to avoid knowing what had happened by simply being satisfied by my father's luck. But that was not enough. My caterpillars were showing me there was something more.

I searched for a map of Nagasaki from 1945. I wanted to know the location of my father's school. He didn't remember the name because he had only been there for three or four months before the bombing and left soon after. He said the school was run by Mitsubishi Heavy Industries and there was a hospital near it. The map showed a promising location: the Mitsubishi Industries Youth School. He said that he entered the school under *gakuto doin* or student mobilization.[4]

Where was the mountain his dormitory was located on? He said that he had crossed a river to get there. But which river?

With the few clues my father gave me seven years earlier, I poured through reports written by atomic-bomb survivors.

は……？　あわてて別なサイトを開き、原爆投下後の長崎の写真を見ていった。広島と同じだ。吐き気がしてきて耐えられなくなり、写真の下にある説明部分だけを読みはじめた。

　そんな逃げ腰状態に陥っていた私の目に、突然、「焼け焦がれた動員学徒」というタイトルが飛び込んできた。動員学徒？　息を殺して写真を見れば、「少年らしきもの」が、うつ伏せになって路上に倒れていた。焼け焦がれて、鉄板にこびりついた肉片のようだった。

　マウスを握りなおすと、白黒の写真を次々とスクロールしはじめた。スピードはどんどん上がっていき、「救援活動をする動員学徒」という写真のタイトルを見たとき、息をのんだ。制服姿の丸坊主の少年が、泥だらけの顔をして写っていた。

　「まさか、父も？　まだ１４歳だったのに……」

　頬を涙が伝った。人間としての父に対して、初めて流した涙だった。

　数日後、実家を訪ねた。

One sentence stood out: *the atomic bomb exploded 500 meters above ground and the resulting flash was seen throughout the area.* I was stunned. My father must be wrong. Even if he had been on the opposite side of the mountain, even if he had been inside the store, he must have seen this flash.

I continued searching. I found a report by a former Mitsubishi Industry employee. It stated workers were ordered to participate in the rescue operation right after the bombing. That means… I quickly opened another site and started looking at the photographs. They showed the same unimaginable human suffering in Nagasaki as in Hiroshima. I started to feel ill; I skipped the images and focused on the captions.

I was about to quit when the words *burnt-out student mobilization* jumped out. Student mobilization? I braced myself and looked at the photograph above the caption. An outline of a boy was lying on the street face down. The body was like a piece of scorched meat on an iron pan.

I started scrolling again through the black and white images. The images passed by faster and faster. Suddenly, a simple title made me catch my breath: *Student mobilization doing rescue work.* The image above the caption was simple: a boy in a school uniform with a shaved head and a muddy face. Was my father forced to do this work? He was just 14 years old.

Tears flowed down my cheeks. This was my first time I cried for my father, not as a parent, but as a human being.

A few days later, I headed home.

Chapter 13

「幼虫は、どうしたの?」

　母がお茶をいれながら言った。

「蝶は毒を持っているって、昔から言われているのよ。子供ができたらどうするの」

　どうも親戚の中に、アゲハ狂いになった私のことを「子供がいないから寂しんだな」と言い出したヤツがいるらしい。

「そういう見方しかできない人間の方が、実は寂しいのよ」

　そう言い返したかったが、今日の私は、そんな暇はない。

「安心してよ。私は、夫の子供以外は生むつもりはないわよ」

　笑いをこらえて、すまし顔で言って返した。

　ところが母は笑うどころか、ぶ然としたので、

「私が育てているナミアゲハは、とっても穏やかなの。毒なんかで武装してないの。びっくりしたら、せいぜい頭からオレンジの角を出すぐらいよ、それが唯一の武器なのよ」

　手を頭において、指を2本立てた。

　幼虫は、頭からオレンジのリボンのようなかわいい臭角を出して、異臭をもつ液体を出す。が、スカンクの一撃にはほど遠く、効果もあまりない。その上、この武器を使い過ぎると、死んでしまうぐらいのお人好しだ。

「イヤだー。気持ちが悪い」

　母は、昆虫が大嫌いだ。

　しかし、世の中は広い。ミカンの木をオンラインで注文したとき、

「幼虫を育てているので、新鮮な葉がたくさんついた木をお願いします」と頼んだのだが、その木が届いた時、カードもついていた。

「拝啓、毎度、お買い上げ頂き、どうもありがとうございます。アゲハが好きな方が結構いまして、今年も多くの方に、ミカンの木を購入していただいております。幼虫がモリモリ葉を食べて、美しいアゲハになりますように。敬具」

Chapter 13

"How are your caterpillars doing?" my mother asked as she made tea.

"You know, butterflies have been said to be poisonous since the old days," she remarked. "What happens if you get pregnant?"

According to her, a few relatives said that I am infatuated with swallowtails because I feel lonely without children. I really wanted to tell her that those people who look at my behavior from that point of view are truly the lonely ones.

However, I had a far more important mission this day and no time for gossip. Instead, I said, "don't worry. I have no intention to give birth to anyone's children but my husband's." Trying not to burst into laughter, I looked at her with a straight face. She was not amused.

"My babies, my swallowtails, are very gentle creatures. They are not armed with poisonous weapons. If they are in danger, they only stick tiny orange antennae out from their heads. That's all they have." I put my hands to my forehead and flicked my index fingers out in imitation.

When threatened, swallowtail caterpillars can emit a pungent odor by using their cute, orange ribbon-like antennae. Sadly, the odor isn't foolproof; nothing like the nasty, foul substance skunks spray. And if they use this deterrent too often, they can die of exhaustion. This is as violent as they come.

"Disgusting! It gives me the creeps," she winced. My mother hates all bugs—no exceptions.

However, the world is always bigger than our imagination. I told her of an online order I had placed for a citrus tree. I had specifically requested a tree with new foliage for my caterpillars. The order came with a card attached to it:

　このカードを読んだとき、優しい余韻で心が溶けてしまいそうだった。私の小さなバルコニーが、外のコミュニティーとつながったように感じた。一方、この話を聞いた母の方は、「世の中も変わったもんねぇ」と、自分の娘以外にも変人がいると知って安心したようだった。

　そこで、私は本題に入らせてもらった。

　「お父さんに、原爆の話を聞いてもいい？　知りたいことがあるの。アメリカがイラクに宣戦布告する前は、アメリカの義母や友人から、反戦のメールがたくさん来ていたのに、戦争が始まったら、全く来なくなったの。恐いね。開戦してしまったら、お終いなんだね。後戻りなんて、できないんだね。だから参考までに、お父さんの話を聞きたいと思って」

　嘘である。先日に夫がつぶやいたことを、無断拝借した。他には、切り札を持っていなかった。

　「お姉ちゃんだって、もっと知りたいってさ」

　これも嘘である。彼女は、二人の息子の子育てで忙しい。父の長崎の話をした時、夫や私のように、寝耳に水といった感じで仰天しつつも、「ラッキーな人ね〜」で終わってしまった。それ以来、この話を持ち出したことはない。

　「いいわ。あの人は、戦後は自分なりにいい人生をおくってきたと思っているから、今なら聞いても大丈夫でしょう。なんでも聞きなさい」

　母は、自らが私の挑戦を受けてたつかのように、真顔で言った。それならば、

　「お母さんは、いつ長崎の話をお父さんから聞いたの？」

　このことが、ずっと気にかかっていたのだ。母は下を向くと、ささやくような声で言った。

　「結婚してすぐ」

　二人はお見合い結婚だったので、この答えを、ある程度は予想していた。さあ、私は母の危険地帯に入った。地雷を踏まずに、父までたどり着かなければいけない。娘として持てるだけの知恵をもって

These kind words moved me to believing that my tiny
balcony had become connected to a larger community
outside. My mother seemed to be relived by this story as well:
her daughter isn't the only weird human in this world.

"Well, the world has changed," she remarked.

With this over, I decided to move on to the reason for my
visit.

"Do you mind if I ask dad about his atomic-bomb
experience? I want to know more. Before America had
declared war on Iraq, my mother-in-law and her American
friends had kept sending us anti-war emails. But once it
started, they stopped. That scared me. Once war starts, there
is no going back. I really want to know his story for the
future."

That was a lie. My husband had commented on that the
other day. I borrowed it since I didn't have a better way to
approach my mother.

"My sister wants to know more about it, too."

Another lie. When I told her our father's story, she was
utterly shocked and amazed with his luck as my husband
and I were, but, being busy with raising two boys, she never
spoke about it since.

"All right," my mother sighed. "He thinks that he has
had a good life since the war. It will be all right now. Just ask
whatever you want to know." She gave me a very serious, but
understanding look as if taking on this challenge herself. So,
I started with her.

"When did you know about his time in Nagasaki?" This
question had been bothering me for sometime.

考えた策は、父を責めて母の複雑な感情を逆なでしないように、慎重に言葉を選ぶことだった。ところが、

「びっくりしたでしょう……」

不覚にも、ぽろりと出てしまった。慎重もへったくりもありゃしない。しかもため息まじりになって、言葉が続かない。

母は、そんな私をしぶい顔をして見ると、おもむろに言った。

「でもね、あの人が『大丈夫だ』って言ったから、それを信じて生きていこうと決めたのよ。あなたがあの話を持ち出すまでは、長崎の話をしたこともなかったわ」

「一度も？」

「ええ」

母の顔には、その決意の深さをほのめかす、不気味な笑みが浮かんでいた。何かと言えば父を責める母にしては、珍しいことだ。母には、もう何も聞かないほうがいい……。

She looked down and murmured, "right after our marriage."

Because they had an arranged marriage, I had anticipated this answer to a certain degree. Now, I entered a minefield. I had to be careful so I could reach my father. With all the wisdom of being her daughter, I had to choose my words carefully as not to inflame any tangled emotions by criticizing her husband. However, that was not what came out of my mouth:

"You must have been shocked."

This was not in my original plan, but that was all I could manage. It was also punctuated with a deep sigh.

She gave me a sour look and slowly said, "he said he was fine. I decided to believe him and move on. Until you brought this up, we had never talked about it."

"Never?"

"No."

She had a slight smile, displaying her commitment to him. This was an unusual confession as my mother blames my father for everything. I better not prod her further.

Chapter 14

父のいる居間に行くと、母は私の後についてきた。私と一緒に、テーブルをはさんで父と向かい合った。

「お父さん、長崎の話を聞きたいの。いいかな?」

聞きながら返事も待たずに、インターネットのサイトからプリントした地図を、父の前に広げた。

「いいよ。でも、覚えているかな」

父は眼鏡をかけると、前屈みになって地図をのぞきこんだ。案外、平気そうである。

「ここ?」

私は、地図上の学校を指した。

「いや、ちがう」

「じゃ、これ? 三菱青年学校?」

「それかもしれない。しかし、よくこんな地図を見つけてきたな」

父の声は、なつかしみを帯びて明るかった。しかし、予想はしていたとはいえ、爆心地から600mぐらいしか離れていない学校の印をみて、こちらは唖然。一呼吸してから、質問を再開した。

「じゃ、寮があった山はどれ?」

父は、地図を近くに引き寄せて、

「橋を渡ったんだから……それから登って……ダメだ、これに載ってないよ」

「寮の名前を思い出せない?」

「3、4ヶ月ぐらいしか、いなかったんだ。忘れたよ」

父の顔色をうかがいながら、ずっと気になっていたことを聞いた。

「かき氷を買ったお店で、ピカっとか、光とか見なかった? 原爆が落ちたのに、気がつかなかったの?」

父は、驚いて遠くを見るように目を見開いたと思ったら、大きな瞬きをした。

「そうだ、そうだ、最初に光ったと思ったら、いきなりドカーンとき

Chapter 14

I entered the living room with my mother right behind me. We both sat at the table across from my father.

"Dad, I want to know more about your experiences in Nagasaki. Do you mind?" Without waiting for his answer, I started spreading out the map that I printed from the internet.

"No, but I wonder if I still remember." He put on his glasses and bent over the map. Unexpectedly, he looked unfazed by the intrusion.

Pointing to the map, I continued, "was this your school?"

"No, not that."

"How about this? Mitsubishi Industries Youth School?"

"That could be it! This is a really old map. Where did you find it?"

His voice had the warmth of nostalgia. I, on the other hand, was stunned. Even though I expected I was right, this school was only 600 meters away from ground zero. After a pause, I continued.

"Where is the mountain your dormitory was located on?"

He moved the map closer to inspect it.

"I crossed a river…and then climbed up a road. No, it is not here, not on this map."

"Do you remember your dormitory name?"

"I was only there for three or four months. I don't."

Watching his face, I asked a question which had been bothering me.

"At the store where you bought the shaved ice, didn't you see a flash? You really didn't notice anything suggesting that a bomb exploded?"

He looked startled. His eyes opened as if looking far away. He then blinked.

"Yes, yes. Now I remember. First, there was a big flash and then a big bang. The windows of the store shattered and salt flooded around my feet."

て、店の窓が粉々に割れたんだ。塩が足下になだれこんできた」
　やっぱり……、7年前の父の話と、すでにだいぶ違うではないか。山登りの途中で雨雲を見つけたときのような不安が、心に広がってきて、
　「塩？　氷じゃないの？」と的外れな質問をすれば、
　「かますが、積んであったんだ」
　父の方は記憶が触発されたらしく、生き生きして答えた。
　「かます？」
　「昔はな、かますっていうのに塩が入っていたんだ」
　「なんでかき氷屋に、塩があるわけ？」
　「雑貨屋みたいなところで、なんでも売っていたんだ」
　いくら話をはぐらかそうとしても、父の心は、あの日あの時にロックされていた。
　「そうだ。あのあと急に何をか感じて、首に手を当ててみたら」
　父の手が、自然に首筋に動いた。
　「手に、血がついているじゃないか。『やられた』と一瞬、思った。そうしたら横にいた子が、けたたましい声をあげて泣き出したんだ」
　同じようにかき氷を買いにきていた男の子がいて、その子の腕から血が飛び散っていた。ガラスの破片で、やられたらしい。父は幸運なことに、厚い制服を着ていたから怪我をしなかった。ただ、その子の血を、顔中にあびた。父はその子の手を引いて、必死に防空壕まで走ったという。
　「中に入ったら人がたくさんいて、その子を取り囲んで介抱しはじめたよ。近所の子だったんだろうな」
　「助かったかな、その子？」
　私がつぶやくと、
　「軽動脈を、やられていたみたいだったから。かわいそうになあ。7、8歳ぐらいだったかな」
　父は下を向いて、黙ってしまった。母も、沈黙している。
　父は今でも、身長が163㎝ぐらいしかない小柄な人だ。その父

As I expected, his story was different from what he
had told me seven years earlier. I was getting nervous, as if
spotting dark clouds over a mountain during a climb.

"Salt? Why not ice?" His answer confused me and I
started deviated from my script.

"There was a large pile of *kamasu.*"

His memories seem to be coming back. He was visibly
excited.

"What is *kamasu?*"

"In those days, salt was stored in a straw bag called a
kamasu."

"Why was salt in a store that sold shaved ice?"

"It was like today's convenience store and sold everything."

I wanted to change the direction of our conversation, but
my father was focused on that day.

"Yes, at the time, I felt something strange. I put my hand
on my throat and then noticed my hand was covered with
blood." He instinctively put his hand to his throat, as if
reliving the moment.

"For a moment, I thought I was done for. And then a boy
standing right next to me started screaming and crying."

That boy was in the store buying shaved ice at the same
time as my father. Blood ran down his arm. He was hit by
window glass scattered by the blast. But, luckily, my father
was protected by the thick material of his school uniform:
the blood on my father's face was the boy's. He grabbed the
boy's hand and set off for an air-raid shelter.

"The shelter was packed when we arrived. People came up
to the boy and started taking care of him. He was probably a
local."

"I wonder if he survived." I murmured.

"His artery seemed to be cut. I felt sorry for him. He was
probably just seven or eight years old."

My father looked down and became silent. My mother
was quiet too.

　が、たった14歳の坊主がりの父が、7、8歳の少年をつれて山道を
逃げる姿を想った。その子も救おうと走った父が、ともて誇らしく思
え、心なぐさむ思いがした。
　「寮へ帰るまで、町が燃えていることに、全く気がつかなかった
の?」
　「もちろん気がついたよ。警報が止まったら、急いで防空壕から
出て町の方を見下ろした。地獄のように燃えていたよ」
　「夜、寮で怖くなかった? 帰ってきた人、少なかったんでしょう?」
　「そんなことはないよ。あの日に学校や工場じゃなくて、遠くの畑
に行っていて、助かった人もいたからな。でも……」
　父は一呼吸をおくと、子供のようにつぶやいた。
　「故郷からいっしょにきた友だちは、死んじゃった」
　「だれ、それ?」
　それまでずっと黙っていた母が、鋭い驚きの声をあげた。
　「いっしょに予科連のテストを受けて落ちた、幼なじみがいたん
だ。二人ともトラホームにかかってしまい、お互いに『おまえがうつし
たから落ちた』って言いあったよ。」
　「その人は、あなたと同じ組にいたの?」
　「ああ、いた。ずっといっしょだった」
　父の表情が、急に暗くなった。私は、母と視線をかわすと、
　「友だちが死んで、辛かったね」
　同情を示したつもりだったが、父は、怒りがこもった冷たい表情を
して、私を見返した。私が、部活や会社を辞めたいというたびに見せ
た、あの表情だ。
　「そんな余裕なんてあるもんか」
　吐き捨てるように言うと、
　「戦争中に、もう、いろいろとやらされて……」
　顔を一瞬ゆがませて、形相を変えた。今だ! と思った。間髪入れ
ずに聞いた。
　「原爆のあと、救援作業をした?」

My father is a small man, around 163 centimeters. I imagined my father as a small 14-year-old boy with a shaved head running for his life with a smaller, wounded seven- or eight-year-old boy in tow down a mountain road. His act of trying to save another life in this chaos made me very proud and I found solace in it.

"On your way back to your dormitory, didn't you notice the town burning at all?"

"Of course! When the air-raid siren stopped, I left the shelter. When I looked down on the town, it was burning with the fires of hell."

"Weren't you scared that night in the dormitory? Only handful people must have come back."

"It was not that bad. That day, some people survived because they were not at school or in the factories. They were working in the fields outside town. But…"

He took a deep breath and, like a small child, said, "my childhood friend who had left our village with me died."

Shocked, my mother broke her silence. Her voice was sharp, "who was he?"

"I had a friend who also applied for the Naval Aviation Preparatory School, We failed together. We were both infected with trachoma. We blamed each other for the infection."

"Was he in your class?"

"Yes. We had been together all this time."

Suddenly, an expression of grief came over my father. My mother and I exchanged glances.

"You must have been sad after his death." I just wanted to show my sympathy, but he rejected it with an icy glance, hiding a deep anger within. Whenever I wanted to quit something I did not like, a school club or job, he would admonish me with that look.

"Who could afford feelings during a war?" he spat out with a tortured face. "During the war, we were forced to do many things…"

　父は、ハッとしたように私を見ると、それまでの興奮が顔から消えた。生気が一気にしぼんで、うなずくように首をたれた。
「えっ?」
　母が、また声をあげた。今度はそれだけでは止まらなくなり、私に取って代わった。
「あなた、行ったの?」
「そりゃ～、行かなくちゃ」
「いつから、かり出されたの?」
「翌日だったかな。それから終戦までの短い間だったけどな」
　母が、怖々と聞いた。
「いったい、何をさせられたの?」
　父は、母と私を交互に見てから、ぼそっと言った。
「……死体集め」

This was the moment for my question, "after the bomb, did you go down to the city and rescue people?"

He stared at me with surprise. His face went blank. He hung his head in resignation.

"What?" my mother interjected, raising her voice. Now, she took over the interview.

"Did you? Really?"

"I had to go."

"When were you called in for the rescue?"

"The day after the bomb hit the city. And until the end of the war. It was a short time."

With trepidation, my mother asked, "what were you forced to do?"

Looking at my mother and me, his words were blunt.

"Collect dead bodies."

Chapter 15

次の日の朝、少年は、救助のために山を下りた。いつもみんなと通った道には、死体が並んでいた。そんな中を、兵隊のあとについて死体を焼却した。死体はどれも、無惨な姿だった。それまで空襲を受けたことがなかった少年にとっては、よもやこの世にあるとは思ってもみなかった光景だった。

　死体の中を、家族の名前を呼びながら、人がさまよっていた。見分けもつかないような死体を焼こうとすると、「身内だから焼かないでくれ」と、自らも余命幾許もないような人たちが、泣いてすがってきた。それが、何よりもつらかった。

　少年は死に引きずられまいと、黙々と死体を運んだ。自分の汗にまじって、服や手に残る他人の肉片、血痕、悪臭……。これが戦争というものなんだと、自分に言い聞かせようとした。

　半壊した建物の中へ入ったときだった。男性が居眠りでもしているかのように、机に突っ伏していた。

　「よかった、まだ生きている」

　少年は、声をあげて駆けよった。しかし、肩に触れたとたん、衣類や皮膚が自分の手の中でくずれ、床にぽろぽろと落ちた。

　「グズグズするな。死体を集めて焼くんだ」

　兵隊の声が、背後から響いた。少年は、男性の屍を椅子から引きずり下ろした。

　「あっ！」

　目を疑った。死人の腕に、見たこともないような高級な腕時計がはめられていた。当時はなんでも没収され、こんなものを持っているだけでも珍しいというのに、その時計は、原爆の熱線や爆風に壊れることなく形をとどめていた。しかも、動いているように見えた。

　「まだ、生きている……」

　時計を見るやいなや、まわりが消えた。文字盤の上を円を描いて動く秒針を、だたただ目で追った。

Chapter 15

The following morning, the boy was sent down the mountain to the city for the rescue operation. Dead bodies lined the same road that he and his friends had taken to school. With a squad of soldiers, he collected and cremated corpses from this landscape. The bodies were unrecognizable. For a boy who had yet to experience an air raid, the landscape he moved through was unimaginable.

People wandered through the remains of the city, calling out to their relatives among the dead. People, who themselves were dying, would approach him. They grabbed his arms, pleading, "don't burn him. He is family." That was the most painful for the boy.

In that chaos, the boy carried the dead in silence, trying not to be overwhelmed by the carnage around him. The human flesh, blood, and stench on his uniform and hands mixed with his sweat. He tried to convince himself that this was somehow normal because it was war.

Entering a half-destroyed building, he found a man leaning forward on his desk as if asleep.

With relief, he broke his silence, "thank god, he's alive." The boy approached him. Touching the man's shoulder, his clothes and skin crumbled onto the floor.

"Don't dawdle. Collect the body and burn it," barked a soldier behind him. The boy dragged the man's body from the chair.

Something caught his eye. An expensive watch was still strapped to the man's wrist. Expensive objects were usually confiscated, making this a rare sight. What surprised him more was the watch appeared to be in perfect shape in spite of the heat from the blast. And whether imagined or true, it appeared to be moving. *Still alive*, he thought. The world around him disappeared. His eyes were transfixed on the second hand drawing an arc across the face of the watch.

　果たして、どれぐらいそうしていたのか？　時計に目が釘付けになっていて、兵隊が後ろからやってくるのに気がつかなかった。
　「この野郎、盗人が」
　兵隊がいきなり殴りかかってきて、少年は床に倒された。兵隊は、執拗に少年の小さなからだを蹴り、彼はただ、死体の横で身を丸めるしかなかった。みんな狂っている……これまで必死に抑えてきたものが嗚咽した。
　「殺すなら、殺せ」
　そのとき、突然、空襲警報が鳴った。兵隊の足が止まったので、少年がうっすらと目を開けると、死体から時計をとって、ポケットに入れる兵隊の姿が見えた。そして身をひるがえすと、防空壕へと走っていってしまった。まわりからも、死体を放り投げて走っていく音がした。遠のいていく足音を聞きながら、少年はよろよろと立ち上がった。
　「急げ、安全な場所に逃げるんだ」

　やっとの思いで近くの防空壕に着けば、中は人であふれていた。少年はその中に一人、身を沈めた。
　「水を……水をくれ」
　薄明りの中で、声がした。目を凝らして見れば、からだ半分を乗り出した状態で、被爆した男性が横たわっていた。青年学校で、誰からも恐れられていた男性教師だった。
　少年の背後から、うす笑う生徒の声が聞こえてきた。
　「あんなやつ、だれが助けるもんか。この間、床につばをはいて、俺に『なめろ』なんて言いやがった。いいきみだ」
　少年は顔をそむけると、目を閉じて体を丸めた。

How long did he stare at the watch? He had no idea. Lost in this vision, he did not notice the soldier approach him.

"Thief!" The soldier hit the boy to the ground and began kicking him repeatedly. Lying next to the dead man, all the boy could do was to curl up his body to protect himself—*was everyone mad?* Finally, he could no longer control himself, sobbing, "if you want to kill me, kill me!"

Suddenly, an air-raid siren sounded. The soldier stopped. The boy opened his eyes and saw him take the watch off the body and put it in his pocket. The soldier then turned and ran for shelter.

The boy heard the sound of people dropping the bodies they were carrying and leave. When the footsteps faded, the boy stood up, still unsteady from the beating. His only thought was to run for safety.

When he finally reached a shelter, it was full. Finding a small space, he slumped down on the ground.

He heard a voice in the dark. "Give me water, water…" He stared in the direction of the voice and saw a man suffering from radiation sickness trying to lift himself up. The boy recognized him. He was one of the teachers at his school. All the students feared him.

He heard another voice sneering, "who would help such a man? Do you know what he did the other day? He spat on the floor and ordered me to lick it up. He deserves this."

The boy turned his eyes away, curling up his body into a ball.

Chapter 16

　私と母は、言葉もなくただ黙っていた。
　「その先生を助ける人は、いなかったよ」
　父が、顔をしかめて言った。
　「もっとも、水はあげられなかった。寮から救助に向かうとき、『水をあげないように』って言われて、それだけは覚えていたから」
　「田舎からいっしょに出てきた友人を、翌日、探した？」
　私だったら、まず一番に探すだろうと思ったから聞いたのだが、父はうつむくと、顔をゆがめて首を振った。
　「学校にはまわされず、他の場所にまわされたよ」
　一瞬だったが、今にも泣き出しそうな悲しい幼子の表情をした。こういう父を、初めて見た。母がそんな父を見て、いたわるように言った。
　「東京大空襲の後に、学生が死体集めにかり出されて、その経験がトラウマとなって、戦後もたいへんだったって聞いたけど……そう、あなたもやらされたのね」
　「ああ。死体を運んでいると、毎日米軍機がやってきた。上を何回も旋回するんだ。でも、攻撃はしてこなかった。『なぜだろう？』って、当時はみんな思ったんだが、あれはその後の様子を観察していたんだな」
　父は、今になって腑に落ちたというような表情をみせた。
　前もって調べておいたのだが、入市被爆者（原爆投下から8月23日までに爆心地から概ね2km圏内に入った者）として、または死体の処理及び救護にあたった者として、父には被爆者手帳を申請する資格があった。ところが、その話を持ち出すと、
　「そんなことするもんか。大丈夫だ。被爆はしていない」
　古傷に触れられた狼のような、鋭くキッとした表情をした。「俺の人生に何をするつもりだ」と、一喝されたも同然だった。
　父の記憶によれば、死体収集作業は終戦の8月15日まで続き、

Chapter 16

My mother and I sat in silence.

My father was sullen. "Nobody helped the teacher. Besides, we couldn't give him water. Before we left the dormitory, we had been expressly told not to give anyone water. That was the only instruction I remembered."

"Did you look for your friend the next day? The friend who left the village with you?" If I had been there, I would have looked for him first.

He looked down and shook his head with a grimace.

"We were ordered to go somewhere else, not to school."

For a moment, I saw in him a helpless boy who wanted to cry. I have never seen him like this.

Acknowledging his pain, my mother pensively added, "I heard that right after the bombing of Tokyo, students were called in to collect dead bodies. The experience was traumatic and they suffered from PTSD long after the war. But I never thought you were called in to do that, too."

"Yes, I was. Every day when I was carrying the bodies, American airplanes came and circled around us. They never bombed us. At that time, we all wondered why. But now I realize that they were observing the effects of the bomb."

He seemed to have found a sensible answer for the strange behaviors of the US airplanes a long time ago.

Before this visit, I found out that my father is qualified to receive an atomic-bomb victim record book. Anyone who entered the city within two kilometers from ground zero between August 9th and 23rd to dispose of bodies or participate in the rescue response were qualified. I suggested he apply for it.

He gave me a sharp look like a wolf whose old wound was touched. "I will do no such thing. I am fine. I was not exposed to radiation." It was as if he thundered, *don't mess with my life!*

その後すぐに故郷に戻されたという。その時にお弁当と電車賃をもらったが、全く十分ではなかった。しかも、長崎から鹿児島までの途中で、何ヶ所も鉄橋が破壊されていたため、3日間ぐらい線路沿いを歩いて帰ったという。

「途中の畑でさつまいもを見つけて、かぶりついたら、歯がぐらぐらして血だらけになった。驚いた。長い間、固いものを食べていなかったことに、自分でもそのとき始めて気がついたよ」

父が、あごのあたりに右手をおいて笑った。

鹿児島の家に着くと、家族のものは驚いたどころではなかった。父が予科練のテストのために鹿児島市内に向かってすぐに、海軍航空隊や予科練がある地域は、ひどい空襲を受けた。家族は、この空襲で父が亡くなったとばかり思っていたらしい。父は、家族と全く連絡をとっていなかったので、父が健康診断で試験に落ちて長崎に向かったことなど、想像だにしていなかったという。

家に戻っても、父にはしなければいけないことがあった。原爆でなくなった幼友達のことを報告する義務を感じて、自ら彼の家を訪ねた。友達の家族は、子供の死に心を痛めながらも、父が生き残ったことを喜んでくれたという。

「あれは、つらかったなぁ」

苦笑いを浮かべて、父が呟いた。

「たいへんだったね。まだ、子供だったのに……」

私が知らず知らずのうちに、テーブルの上の父の手に手をのばすと、父は観念した子供のようにうなずいた。

He continued with rescue work and body disposal until
August 15th, the end of the war, before being permitted
to return home. He was given some food and money for
transportation. But it was insufficient for the journey.
Between Nagasaki and Kagoshima, a number of bridges had
been destroyed. He spent about three days following the rail
lines on foot.

"On my way, I found a sweet potato field and took some
to eat. But, when I took a bite, my teeth started bleeding and
were loose." He raised his right hand to his jaw. "I realized
that it had been a long time since I had solid food."

When he arrived home, to say his family was overjoyed to
see him would be an understatement. Not long after he set
out for Kagoshima city to enter the Japanese Naval Aviation
Preparatory School, his family received the news the school
was destroyed in an air raid. Since my father had not told his
family that he failed the physical and left for Nagasaki, they
assumed he died in the raid.

But this was not the end to his story. There was one more
thing he had to do. He thought that it was his duty to report
the death of his friend to his family in person. His friend's
family was sad to learn of his death, nevertheless, they were
grateful that my father survived.

"That was really tough," my father murmured with a
bitter smile.

"Dad, you had been through a lot, especially since
you were just 14." Spontaneously, I reached out and took
his hand resting on the table. With a nod like a child, he
resigned himself to his past.

Chapter 17

バルコニーは今、夏の盛りを迎えて、蛹と幼虫の天下となっている。3年の間に、7㎡もないバルコニーに18本のミカン科の木が並んだ。どうやったら収まったのか、自分でも不思議だ。そんな木々を満足げに見ては、空を見る。14歳の少年の頃の父を想像してみる。数日前に父から聞いた長崎の体験は、私の知らない父、別な人間を私の中に生んだ。

　父は、子育ては母に任せっきりで、子供とはあまり会話をしてこなかった。ただ選挙になると、「投票に行かないのか？　お前は、バカだ。大事なことだ。投票に行け」と、私を叱った。今は、この言葉の真意が痛いほどわかる。どうして、耳を傾けなかったのか。

　また、私が相談をすれば、いつも返ってくる「そんなことで、世の中生きていかれるか」という、役立たずで腹立たしい助言が、今は「大丈夫だ。なんとかなる」という、父なりの励ましの言葉だったとわかる。もっと前に、長崎での体験を話してほしかった。

　それに、父が沈黙を破ったことで、一つの謎がとけた。戦争とは全く関係のない事だが、なぜ私の赤ん坊の時の写真がないのかわかった。

　私の目が見えないかもしれないと医者に言われたとき、長崎での父の被曝が、その原因として二人の心の中に真っ先に上がってきたに違いない。母は、結婚前に長崎の事を言わなかった父を、暗黙のうちに非難しつづけ、父は、かたくなに長崎の事を考えまいと否定しつづけ、自分の過去から逃げるために、逆に母を責めていたかもしれない。二人は、私の写真を撮るまでの1年の間、麻痺した時間を過ごしたのだろう……。これで、やっと二人を許せる。

Chapter 17

By midsummer, my balcony is a world of caterpillars and
chrysalises. It is amazing to see 18 citrus trees in a 75 square
foot space. How could I manage to do this? I look at my
trees with a sense of accomplishment. I gaze up at the sky
and imagine my father as a 14-year-old boy. For the past few
days, thinking about his experience in Nagasaki, a new man
is being created in my mind.

He left child raising to my mother, seldom communicating
with his children. However, whenever there was an election,
he would chide, "why don't you go and vote? You are an
idiot. Voting is essential. Go vote!" Now I understand and
am ashamed of not listening to him.

On the occasion I would ask for help, he always gave me
the typical useless, irritating advice that parents give, "how
could you live in this world with such an attitude? You are
too spoiled." However, now I see that as encouragement, as
if to say, *don't worry. It will be all right.* I wish that he could
have told me his story a long time ago.

Another mystery was solved through his story. Not about
the war, but the lack of my baby photos.

The doctor's prognosis of my blindness must have affected
my parents greatly. Given my father's experience in Nagasaki,
I am sure that they thought that radiation exposure could
have been the reason for my health. My mother could
have secretly blamed him for not telling her before their
marriage. On the other hand, with my father's denial of that
experience, he could have blamed my mother for my white
eyes. They must have had a paralyzing year of uncertainty. As
for me, I can finally forgive them.

Chapter 18

はやる心を抑えて、今朝もゆっくりとカーテンを開ければ、バルコニーのミカンの木に、アゲハがとまっている。細長い足で、枝から逆さにぶら下がっている。その横には、もぬけの殻となった蛹がある。昨日、蛹が透き通ってきたので、前もってネットをとっておいてよかった。まだ蛹の中には体液が残っているから、出てきて間もないにちがいない。

　これからおよそ2時間、アゲハは、ぶら下がったままだろう。しわくちゃな羽をのばし、乾くのをじっと待つ。そして、空へと羽ばたいていく。

　この3年で100頭以上のアゲハを空に放ってきたが、その大半が、朝に旅立っていった。他の太った幼虫も、もうすぐ蛹となり、9月に羽を広げて去っていくだろう。

　9月にバルコニーで生まれた幼虫の旅は、春や夏生まれのものよりも長い。蛹となって、冬をここで越すからだ。氷点下の日、バルコニーの隅でひっそりとしている命を思いやってみる。虫と共に冬を越しているという実感が、私を優しくしてくれる。小さな生き物とつながっていると思うだけで、自分の息すらも、細やかな虫の息のように感じる。

　そして、なんといっても彼らが3月に美しい蝶となり、第一陣として飛び立っていくときのうれしさよ。まだ風が冷たく、桜も咲いていないときに、旅立ちの命を受けたものたち。それを見送るとき、私の心は、命への畏敬の念にあふれる。

　　さあ　いっておいで　春の申し子たち
　　春風を味方につけて　舞っておいで

　目の前で起きている事が奇跡でないのなら、この世に奇跡など存在しないとすら思えてくる。

Chapter 18

Resisting the urge to throw open the curtain, I slowly draw it back to peer onto the balcony. Just as I expected, a butterfly is hanging upside down from its long, thin legs on a branch of a potted orange tree. Next to it, an empty chrysalis. The day before, the chrysalis turned transparent, foretelling the arrival of this morning's visitor and prompting me to remove the net from around the tree. The liquid remaining in the shell of the chrysalis meant the butterfly emerged just moments before.

The swallowtail will hang there for about two hours, patiently unfurling and drying its wings. Hopefully, they will carry it away into the world.

For the past three years, I have raised more than one hundred of these intrepid swallowtails. Most follow a morning departure schedule. The remaining chubby caterpillars on the balcony will very soon become chrysalises and emerge as butterflies, leaving in September.

Any eggs hatching in September have a longer journey. They will spend the coming winter with me as chrysalises. On cold winter days, when the temperature dips below zero, knowing that I am journeying through the winter with these small creatures makes me kinder and gentler. I feel like my breath is as faint as theirs.

When a new cycle begins in March, seeing them leave as beautiful swallowtails is a joy. They are the brave ones who have a mission to fly when the wind is still cold and the cherry trees have yet to bloom. Seeing them off into the sky, I am in awe of life.

Go, child of spring.
Win over the spring wind and dance with it.

If what is happening in front of me isn't a miracle, then miracles don't exist in this world.

Chapter 19

朝、父から電話があった。父から電話が来たことなどないので、母に何かあったのかとあわてれば、
　「あのな、電話をしたのは、思い出したからだよ」
　うれしそうな声をしている。
　「何を?」
　「長崎にいたときの寮の名前だよ。知りたがっていただろう? 平戸小屋寮だ[4]。学校が終わると『さあ、平戸小屋に帰ろう』って、みんなで言いあったもんだった」
　「いったいどうやって思い出したの?」
　「昨日、戦争映画を見たんだよ。幼い兄妹が爆撃を受けたときに、塩が積んであったかますの後ろに、身をふせて隠れるシーンがあってな。自分も、とっさに同じ事をしたから」
　「でも、寮とは関係のないシーンなのにね」
　「そうなんだけど、当時の記憶がよみがえった。60年ぐらいも前のことなのにな。あったことは脳が全部、記憶しているって聞いたけど、本当だな」
　照れを隠す笑い声になっている。きっとまた、頭をかいているにちがいない。
　「不思議だね。戦争中の夢なんて、見ないんでしょう?」
　「今は見ないけど、戦後は数年間、よく見たよ。いやーなもんだった」
　「ごめんね。思い出させてしまったかもしれない」
　「そんなことないよ。まあ、元気でな」
　やさしい声だった。それだけに、無性にやるせなくなってきた。なぜ父という人間が、地獄のような経験をしなければならなかったのか、私にはわからない。人間の天敵が、他の人間なんてことがあっていいはずながない。
　電話を切ると、私の足はバルコニーへと向かった。私の小さな森、小さな天国。

Chapter 19

One morning, I received a call from my father. Since he seldom calls his daughters, I was worried that something had happened to my mother.

"I am calling you because I remembered now." His voice sounded pleasant.

"Remember what?"

"The name of the school dormitory in Nagasaki. You wanted to know, didn't you? It was Hirado Goya. When school ended, we used to say to each other, 'let's go back to Hirado Goya.'"[5]

"Why did you suddenly remember?"

"Last night, I was watching a war movie on TV. There was a scene where a young brother and a sister hid themselves behind a supply of salt when they were being bombed. I did the same thing."

"But the scene has nothing to do with your dormitory."

"That's right, but it triggered my memories of that time. I hear that our brain remembers everything we experience. Now I know that it is true." He laughed as if to hide his embarrassment. He must be scratching his head again.

"That's interesting. You haven't had any dreams related to the war, have you?"

"Not now, but, for a few years after the war, I did. They were horrible."

"I am sorry, dad. Did I bring back those nightmares?"

"Not at all. Anyway, take care."

His voice was full of gentleness. Yet, I was despondent. I could not reconcile this person with the cruelty of his experience. The natural enemy of humans should not be other humans.

Hanging up the phone, I went out to the balcony. My small forest became a small heaven.

Chapter 20

いつものように幼虫や蛹の数を数え終えて、ふと視線を上げると、アゲハが１頭、こちらへ一直線に飛んでくる。「まあ、新しいお客様」と思ったが、どこか飛び方がおかしい……。激しく羽ばたきながら、必死に飛んでくる。よく見れば、後ろの羽が１枚ない。鳥にでも食べられそうになったところを、危うく逃げ切ったのだろう。

バルコニーにたどり着くと、ネットがかかった木に卵を生もうとして、うろうろしはじめた。最後の力を振り絞っているかのようだった。

「こっちに早く、早く」

柔らかい若葉の多い木のネットを取り払うと、すぐに部屋の中に入って、窓越しにアゲハを見つめた。

アゲハは、かぼそい脚で葉を確認すると、卵を一つ一つ丁寧に生みはじめた。この世界で恐い経験をしたというのに、それでも必死に卵を産んでいく。本能に操られ、進化の気が遠くなるような長い時間に、身をゆだねることしかできないのか。

「安心して産んでおいき」慰めるような気持ちで呟いた。

おそらくこのバルコニーで育った蝶が、卵を産むために戻ってきたのだろう。蝶は１年で２〜５世代生まれるらしいから、３年目の今では、最初の蝶から数えて15世代目ぐらいが、このバルコニーで誕生している可能性がある。

今年は私が顔を近づけても、幼虫が臭角を出してガス攻撃してこない。木から木へ移動させる時も、手のひらの上でじっとしている。脱走しようとせず、おとなしくネットの中で蛹になるものまで出てきた。これぐらいの時がたてば、「このバルコニーは安全地域」という情報が、DNAにしっかりと書き込みされているのかもしれない。

けれども、羽をもぎ取られたアゲハを窓越しに見ながら、混乱してきた。天敵の食性もいっしょに変わらなければ、食物連鎖は変わらない。ネットの外に出れば、アゲハが天敵に襲われる可能性は変わらない。いったい私は、何をしているのだろうか？

Chapter 20

One day, after counting my caterpillars and chrysalises, I glanced up and saw a swallowtail flying towards the balcony. *Another visitor*, I thought. But something was strange. The swallowtail was flapping its wings frantically to stay in the air. A part of its lower wing was missing. It must have had a close encounter with a bird.

Once the butterfly landed, it wandered over the nets covering the trees. With this final effort, it had come to lay its eggs.

"Come over here quickly." I removed a net from a tree full of young leaves and retreated into the apartment.

I watched it from the window. The swallowtail checked the leaves with its long, thin legs and started laying eggs. It must have had a terrible journey, but it is laying its eggs. Is that all they can do? Being driven by instinct, they leave their fate to the unimaginable long road of evolution.

"Don't worry. Leave them on this balcony," I whispered.

The swallowtails that grew up here probably return to lay eggs. They repeat this cycle with two to five generations hatching in a season. Assuming the first swallowtails that hatched on my balcony three years ago returned, the current ones could be the fifteenth generation.

This year showed a change in their behavior. No caterpillars have stuck their antenna out in attempts to repel me when I approach them. When I need to move them to another tree, they don't resist when I pick them up and stay perfectly calm on the palm of my hand. Nor do they frantically race in the nets to find a place to become a chrysalis. The swallowtails must know this place is safe. Has the knowledge of this safe environment been written into their DNA?

But, looking at this swallowtail with a missing wing, I am confused. As long as the diet of their natural enemies does not change, this food chain remains the same. Outside the safety of my nets, my swallowtails still face danger from their predators. What in the world am I doing?

Chapter 21

羽化してからのアゲハの命は、せいぜい2、3週間しかない。人間からすれば、数々の試練や変態を生き延びて、やっと蝶になれたというのに、なんとも割の合わない短い虫性だ。だから、幼虫がこのバルコニーにいる間だけでも、安全に暮らさせてあげたいと思うのだろう。

でも私のせいで、のろまな蝶になってしまったらどうしよう。天敵に食べられたり、子供に捕まったり、昆虫採集のためにピン止めされたらどうしよう。放っておいたほうが、アゲハのためだろうか？

いや、蝶族は、こうした私の同情や感傷を笑うかもしれない。なんせ彼らは、2億年も前から生息している。熱帯には、毒をもつ蝶すらいる。「おれが死ぬときは、おまえもいっしょだ」と、その蝶を食べた天敵は、蝶もろとも死ぬ。人間と同じだ。生物というものが、追い詰められると、最終的には共倒れの方向を選んでいくとしたら、どうしてこれを進化といえよう。絶望的だ。

でも、アゲハ保育園は、アゲハのためだけではなく、私のためでもある。父の長崎での本当の体験を知ってから、私は幼虫に、自分自身を見るようになってきた。

たくさんの犠牲のもと、日本は第二次世界大戦後、「恒久平和」という道を選択してくれた。私は、憲法第9条という安全ネットの中に生まれた幼虫の一つなのだ。

幸運なことに、今もネットを縛るヒモを緩めていないから、拳銃の音一つ聞くことなく、これまで安全に暮らしてこられた。最高に幸せなことで、ありがたく思っている。

しかし、それでも私には、得体のしれない不安がいつもある。幼児期から感じていたから、説明がつかない。幼い頃は、今でも記憶に残っているような怖い夢を見て、よく泣いた。8歳ぐらいまでは、工場やパトカーのサイレンが鳴ると、どこにいようが泣きながら家をめざした。夜は、棒を持って家じゅうの戸締りをして歩いた。そんな私を、家族のものはただ「弱虫ねぇ」と笑った。

Chapter 21

A swallowtail's adulthood is a brief span of two to three weeks. From a human standpoint, it seems like an injustice to reach their final form after all the trials and transformations only to live such a short time. Perhaps this is why I have devoted myself to offering them a safe haven.

However, what if my actions result in them becoming stupid or naive? What if my kindness makes them vulnerable to predators, the nets of children, or the traps of collectors? Would it have been better to have left them to their fate?

Or, maybe, they are laughing at my naive sympathy and sentimentality. Butterflies have existed on this planet for about two-hundred-million years. Some tropical butterflies are poisonous, a fatal mistake for anything that preys on them: a strategy of mutually assured destruction used by human beings. If creatures are driven to such an extreme where the only option is to fall together, how is this evolution? How depressing.

But this nursery is not only for my swallowtails, but also myself. Since I learned of my father's experience in Nagasaki, I have started seeing myself in my swallowtails.

At the end of World War II, the Japanese government chose permanent peace because so many innocent human lives were sacrificed. I am one of those caterpillars born under the safety net of Article 9 of the Japanese Constitution.

Fortunately, since then, we haven't loosened that net. I have lived safely without hearing a single shot being fired. This is incredibly lucky. I am so very grateful.

However, an illogical fear is somewhere inside me. I can't explain it. It started when I was an infant. I often cried at night, having bad dreams, some of which I still remember. For the first eight years of my life, I would run home crying whenever I heard police or factory sirens. Every night, armed with a club, I would check every door and window in my

　もしかしたら、父がずっと心の奥深くで押し殺してきたものが、私の中を、我が物顔で歩いているのではないだろうか？　もしそうならば私という人間は、安全ネットの中にいるのに、不安から安全を求めて脱走しようとする幼虫たちと、似たようなものではないだろうか。
　先日、実家を訪ねた時、
「長崎にいたことを、どうして7年前に突然に言ったの？」
　率直に父に聞いたら、
「あれは、つい口が滑ったんだ。『しまった』と思ったよ」
　照れ笑いで返してきた。
　この人は、本当に長崎の体験を、黙って墓場まで持っていこうとしていたのだ。父よ、あなたにとっては、それでよかったかもしれない。でも、それだけでは終わらないものがある……。

house to make sure they were locked. My family just laughed at me. They thought I was just a scaredy-cat.

I wonder if what my father had suppressed so deeply since the war has been acting through me? If that is the case, then I am like my caterpillars that are unaware of the protective net around them and frantically run to seek safety.

During my last visit with my dad, I came straight to the point, "Why did you suddenly tell me about Nagasaki seven years ago?"

"It was, just…it just came out, damn it!" He laughed with embarrassment.

I was shocked to think that he had really been determined to take Nagasaki to his grave quietly. Dad, you might have been all right with it, but that doesn't mean the story ended with you.

Chapter 22

秋が来た。残る幼虫は、6匹だけ。蛹となって、ここで冬を越すものも出てくるだろう。

この3年間、アゲハへの愛情は、強くなっていくばかりだった。虫かごを持っている子供を見ると、「アゲハを捕まえても、逃がしてあげてね」と、お願いをするように言って通り過ぎた。本当は「そこのガキ、アゲハを捕まえるなよ」と言いたかった。

一定期間、アゲハを捕まえるのをやめたら、やがてはアゲハの方から、人間の肩や手に止まってくるような世界がやってくる可能性があることなど、子供にわかるわけがない。この自分だって、3年間にわたって幼虫を育てる経験を通して、初めてそんなことを考えるようになった。

見えない可能性をこの世に出してくるカギは、環境設定と、それを維持する一定の時間なのだ。それなのに、人間の脳内の時間軸は、あまりに短い。

なんか、この秋は虚しい。

Chapter 22

Autumn has arrived. Only six caterpillars are left on my balcony. Some of them will winter with us here.

Over the past three years, my love for swallowtails grew. Whenever I saw a child with an insect cage, I begged them to release any swallowtails they caught. What I really wanted to express was more direct, *kid, leave these butterflies alone!*

For children, a world where butterflies would approach them freely if they stopped hunting them is impossible to understand. But I can't blame them as this would never had occurred to me until I started raising swallowtails.

Perhaps the key to bringing unseen possibilities into this world is to create the right environment and the time for the change to be realized. However, the reality is human timescales are too short.

This autumn, I am feeling powerless.

Chapter 23

私は、歩き慣れた近所の道を、踏切へと向かって歩いていた。すると、右手に大きな鳥居が現れ、上に続く階段が見えた。明らかに、その先に神社があると感じた。

　突然、体が宙に浮いた。何ごとかと足元を見れば、大きな手のひらが見える。巨大な何者かが、私を手のひらに乗せて運んでいるではないか。慌てて見上げれば、見えるのは、巨人の上半身のほんの一部だけ。

　びっくりして手のひらにしゃがみ込むと、私はそのまま、一本の大きな木の方へ運ばれていった。木の枝は、枝垂れ桜のように豊かに大きくしなっていた。しかも、たくさんの種類のフルーツが、枝からぶら下がっていた。珍しい木だった。

　手に乗せられたまま、私は木の真下に運ばれた。声こそしなかったが、好きなフルーツを枝から一つ取るようにと、勧められているのがわかった。

　「とんでもない。私には、もったいなくて」

　恐れ多くなって心の中で遠慮すると、近くの枝にあったバナナを勧められた。

　突然、シーンが変わった。私は、踏切を渡った反対側の町に立っていた。開発が猛スピードで進んでいて、木々がどんどん伐採され、砂埃の向こうにブルドーザーが見えた。

Chapter 23

Walking on a familiar neighborhood street, I approach a railroad crossing. I notice a large torii gate[6] with steps beyond leading up to a shrine that is just out of sight.

I begin floating in the air. Looking down, I see a giant hand lifting me up. A gigantic god is carrying me on his palm. I look up; all I can see is the side of his upper body. Afraid, I collapse onto his palm.

He transports me to a large tree. The branches arc gracefully like a weeping cherry tree. A cornucopia of fruit is hanging from each branch. I have never seen such a tree.

The hand carries me beneath a branch. I understand this voiceless deity is asking me to take any one of the fruit I desire.

"No, you are too generous," I humbly object.

The god recommends that I take the banana hanging near me.

Suddenly, I am standing across from the railroad crossing. The area is being rapidly developed. Trees are being cut down. I see a bulldozer in a cloud of dust.

Chapter 24

珍しい夢を見たものだ。あっという間に終わったし、音もなかった。ともかく鮮烈で、全てを自分の視線で見ていた。

面白いことに、夢の中で歩いていた道は、ここから10分ぐらいの場所で、確かに存在している。踏切の反対側の町も、実在している。ただ、あの道には鳥居なんてない。もちろん、鳥居から上に続く階段もなけば、神社もない。

それに、気になることがあった。夢の最後の部分だ。夢の中で、木がどんどん切られていく風景を見ながら、深い悲しみを感じた。それは、私のものではなかった。あの辺りには、かつてはあんなに木々があったのだろうか。現時点では、ビルがどんどん建てられている。

「だれかが、何かを伝えにきたのだろうか?」

いい年して探偵ごっこじゃないが、まずは、手のひらの主を見つけなくてはいけないような気がしてきた。もちろんこれまでの人生で、そんなことをしたことは一度もない。正直、ちょっと怖い。でも、真実を探ったほうがいい。もし何もなければ、「ほらね。単なる夢だよ」と笑える。

でも、もし何かあったら……どうする? 神社どころか、変なものがあったらどうする? いや、あの道は、店と家でいっぱいだ。考えすぎだ。

こんな押し問答を、一人で延々と繰り返した数週間後、意を決して夢に出たあたりを歩いてみた。やはり道の両側には、家や店しかない。鳥居や神社なんてない。

「私も、相当なひま人だよな～」

自分が滑稽で、顔に薄ら笑いを浮かべ、踵を返そうとした。が、一瞬、足が止まった。家と家の間の1m幅ぐらいの脇道に、小さな赤い祠が祀られていたのだ。左を見れば、50mぐらい先には踏切があり、その向こうには、開発が進んだ地域がある。

呆然とした。これを、どう理解すればいいのだろうか。

Chapter 24

What a strange dream. The vision was short, vivid, and silent. I saw everything as clearly as I would with my own eyes.

Interestingly, the street in my dream actually exists ten minutes from my apartment. The area opposite from the railroad crossing also exists. However, that street has no torii gate…or steps…or shrine.

Something bothered me. At the end of the dream, when seeing the trees being cut down, I sensed a deep sadness. A sadness that was not mine. Were there so many trees in this area before? I could not imagine it with all the new buildings there now.

Was someone sending me a message?

In spite of being old enough to know better, I felt like I had to play detective and find out whose hand carried me. I had never acted on my dreams before. Honestly, I was a bit scared. But, if there is something to it, I should really find out. However, when I confirm there is nothing on that street, I can laugh at myself and my foolish dream.

But I was conflicted: what if there is something there? Not a shrine, but something sinister. As far as I remember, the street is just full of houses and shops. I must just be imagining this.

After a few weeks of indecision, I decide to walk around the neighborhood to put an end to my speculation. Sure enough, on both sides of the street, there are only houses and shops. No torii gate. No shrine. Just as I expected.

I almost start laughing at myself and my useless investigation. As I am about to turn and leave, something stops me. Between two houses, down a four-foot wide path, is a tiny shrine. I look to the left. 60 yards away, a railway crossing. Beyond that, a newly developed area.

I am stunned. What is this?

　こんな小さな祠でも、別次元では、鳥居や階段がある大きな神社なのか。かつては大きかったのに、開発によって今の状況に押しやられたのかもしれない。
　「あの、もしかして？」
　往来の中、一人棒立ちになって祠を見つめた。

In a different dimension, could this small shrine have had a large torii gate and ascending steps? Maybe it had been more extensive at a different time, but was reduced to its current state by human development.

"Excuse me. Are you…by any chance…" Among the crowds on the street, I stand bolt upright, staring at the tiny shrine.

Chapter 25

アパートにもどると、すぐにバルコニーに出た。たった今、見てきたことは、どのようにでも捉えることができる。ただこの世界が、五感を超えた複雑で大きな世界の中にあることは、確かなようだ。私の心は、今、その世界をじっと探ろうとしている。

　五感では感知しえないその世界に、私を認知している存在がいる。しかもその存在は、私に感謝をしている。私が、都会の小さなバルコニーにミカン科の木の森を作って、アゲハを育てているからだろうか？　そういう神秘というか、不可思議があっても、ちっともおかしくない。アゲハが蛹から出てくる瞬間を見た人なら、それがわかる。受け入れられる。

　考えてみれば、夢の中で神様の手のひらに乗って運ばれた私が、この現実世界では、幼虫を自分の手のひらに乗せて運んでいる。私が「神様が、私のために運んでくれた」と感じたように、幼虫も「自分のために運んでくれた」と、私のことを思う（おそらくあり得ないだろうが）かもしれない。そうしたら私は、幼虫の夢の中の神様となる……。私は人間をしながらも、幼虫にでも、神様にでもなりえるのだ。

　面白い。どこか「自分」という縛りが、ほどけていくような気がする。真冬にバルコニーのサナギを思うと、密やかな繋がりを感じて笑みが浮かんでくるが、今、同じ喜びが外へと広がっていく。

Chapter 25

As soon as I return to the apartment, I go out to the balcony. What I have just seen could be interpreted in many ways. But whatever that is, this world seems to belong to a larger, more complex one beyond my perception. My mind seems to be trying to reach into this world and understand.

In that world beyond my five senses, a deity acknowledged me. What is more, this god showed me gratitude. Is this why I have been nurturing orange trees and swallowtails in this big city? This mystery may not be so strange. Those who have ever seen the moment a swallowtail emerges from its chrysalis can understand it, they can accept it.

On reflection, I, who was carried on the palm of a god in a dream, carry caterpillars on my palm in this world. Perhaps, just as I felt the deity acted for my benefit, my caterpillars may feel the same about me (although, unlikely). Maybe I am their god in a caterpillar dream. While I, myself, am living, I could be a caterpillar and a deity.

How strange. This fixed idea of *me* seems to be coming unbound. Whenever I think of hibernating caterpillars passing the winter on my balcony, I smile at this secret connection to them. Now, this same joy is reaching out to the world.

Chapter 26

ネットの外に出たらどうなるの？
ネットの内を広げていれば
そのうちに
「ネットの外」が
消えているかもしれないよ

Chapter 26

What would happen if I leave the net?
By expanding my net
from inside
one day, I may find
the world outside
gone

Notes

Chapter 5

[1] **青年学校:** 1935年の青年学校令によって設立された。尋常小学校(当時の小学校)を卒業した男子は、職業教育と軍事教育、女子は家事裁縫などの教育を受けた。1947年に廃止。

Chapter 6

[2] **予科練:**「海軍飛行予科練習生」及びその制度の略称で、大日本帝国海軍における航空兵養成制度の一つ。志願制で、終戦までの15年間の間、14才半から17才までの約24万人の少年が試験で選抜され、搭乗員としての基礎訓練を受けた。このうち、約2万4千人が戦地へ赴き、戦死者はその8割の1万9千人にのぼった。

Chapter 12

[3] **動員学徒:** 学徒勤労動員(がくときんろうどういん)または学徒動員(がくとどういん)の名の下に、第二次世界大戦末期の1943年、深刻な労働不足を補うために中等学校以上の生徒が、軍需産業や食糧生産に動員された。それらの生徒を、動員学徒と呼んだ。

Chapter 19

[4] **平戸小屋寮:** 飽の浦寮(あくのうらりょう)の記憶違いと思われる。父が最初に入ったのは、三菱長崎工業青年学校の平戸小屋寮(ひらどごやりょう)であることは確かだが、1945年

Notes

Chapter 5

[1] In 1935, students were required to attend Youth Schools after graduating elementary school. Youth Schools were mixed vocational and basic military training for boys and home economics for girls. They were abolished in 1947.

Chapter 6

[2] The Naval Aviator Preparatory Course was established by the Imperial Japanese Navy to train flight crews. Boys between 14 and a half and 17 years old could volunteer. From 1929 to the end of the World War II, 240,000 boys were selected. 24,000 served in combat during the war, of which 19,000, or 80 percent, died.

[3] In Japan, ghosts are believed to have no legs.

Chapter 12

[4] Because of labor shortages in 1943, the Japanese government mobilized students in junior high schools or higher to work in agriculture or the defense industry.

Chapter 19

[5] According to my research, the dormitory my father was heading to on that day was called Akunoura. Even though my father initially lived at Hirado Goya, everyone was moved to Akunoura due to the increasing air raids by the American military. Akunoura dormitory was 3.4 kilometers away from ground zero on Mt. Inasa. That

の春ぐらいから米軍の爆撃機の襲来が増えたので、平戸小屋の寮生は全員、飽の浦寮へと転居したらしい。またこの寮は、爆心地から3.4kmのところにあり、稲佐山（いなさやま）という小高い山が、防御の役目を果たし、爆風や熱線の被害をかなり軽減してくれたという。山が守ってくれたという、父の説明と一致する。

mountain protected residents from the blast and radiation on August 9th, 1945.

Chapter 23

[6] Torii gates, made from two upright pillars capped with two crosspieces, mark the entrance to Shinto shrines.

About the Author

東京でビジネス及び出版翻訳家、衛星放送局でフルタイムの詩人として働いたのち、2006年に夫ウィリアム・アッシュと共にアメリカに移住。自然が豊かなメイン州で１０年間、執筆活動をしながら、自給自足的な暮らしを探求する。同時に小さな出版社「Hakusan Creation」を立ち上げ、東京の独身女性の結婚までの内面の変化を描いた自伝的詩集「乙姫から浦島太郎に告ぐ」を2014年に、3周した四国遍路道の日記をまとめた「空海の人びと」を2016年に出版。現在、ワシントンDC在住。

About the Author

After working in Tokyo as a business and publication translator and a full-time nature poet for a satellite broadcasting station, Naomi moved to the United States with her husband William Ash in 2006. She pursued a self-sufficient life in Maine for ten years, exploring the natural world and writing poetry. During this time, she started a small publisher Hakusan Creation. She has published two other books of her work: "乙姫から浦島太郎に告ぐ" in 2014, an autobiographical poetry book about her psychological journey from a single woman in Tokyo to her marriage, and "空海の人びと" in 2016, a diary of her three experiences of completing Japan's longest walking pilgrimage on the island of Shikoku. Currently, she lives in Washington, DC.

Hakusan Creation: https://www.hakusancreation.com
書籍販売ショップ/Shop: https://hakusan-creation.myshopify.com/
お問い合わせ/Contact: hakusan_creation@me.com

左の写真：2003年、アゲハを育て始める前のバルコニーに立つ著者。

Photo: The author in her balcony garden in 2003, just before the arrival of her butterflies.

英語訳を楽しまれる方へ

英訳は、日本語の原作を一語一語、単純に訳したものではありません。原作の意味を変えることなく、英語のリズムが生かされるように、単語や文章に工夫を凝らしています。英語感覚で訳した英訳をお楽しみください。

About the Translation

The English text from the original Japanese is not a literal
word-for-word translation. To preserve the natural rhythm
of both languages for the reader, each text has slightly
different word choices and sentence structures to capture the
underlying meaning of the story. We hope you enjoy this
very personal project.

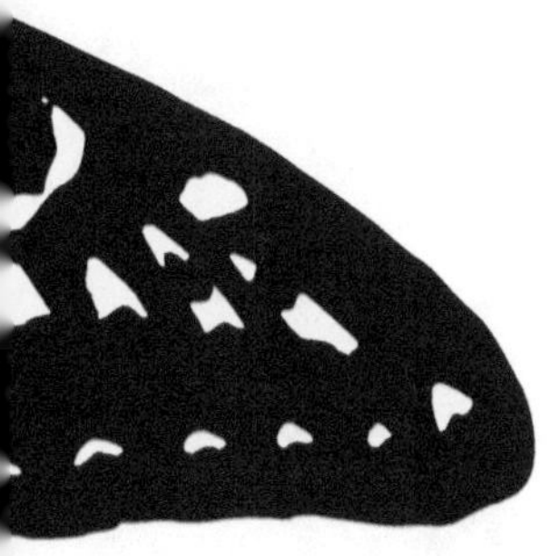